relation of elements
using prepositions to shape design

T0301060

BIS Publishers
Borneostraat 80-A
1094 CP Amsterdam
The Netherlands
T +31 (0)20 515 02 30
bis@bispublishers.com
www.bispublishers.com

ISBN 978 90 636 9686 3

relation of elements
using prepositions to shape design

Ryan Crooks

BISPUBLISHERS

"No house should ever be on a hill or on anything. It should be of the hill. Belonging to it."

-Frank Lloyd Wright

The Preposition Game

Language is an incredible system that is able to encapsulate meaning through the use of words with a known meaning that is shared across the culture. As we learn in school, there are eight parts of speech: articles, nouns, pronouns, verbs, adjectives, adverbs, conjunctions, and prepositions. Articles define the general or specific item; nouns describe the individual or object that is involved in the action of the sentence; pronouns are place markers for nouns; adjectives clarify and qualify the nouns; verbs describe the action; adverbs modify and describe the verb; conjunctions tie the nouns or parts of a sentence together, and prepositions describe the relations of elements.

Many architects feel the verb is the most important part of speech to express the qualities of a building, but architectural elements tend to be passive and it is the inhabitant or user who creates the action within a space –these are the verbs, while the building and its parts are the nouns. Architecture is acted upon. However, when we look at the collection or assembly of parts that make up architecture and architectural spaces, we begin to understand that the form, layout, and the interrelationship of building elements provide the spirit of the structure. This interrelationship is expressed through the preposition.

In school, teachers often explain prepositions through the use of metaphors, such as all the things a rabbit can do with a log or all the ways a plane can interact with a cloud. These are very spatial, and the choice of preposition informs the relationships of a space, agent, or materials. Therefore, it is arguably the most architectural word, however many or most architects look to the verb first. This work is meant to show that the preposition is a very useful part of speech to study and use, and it can create new forms and relationships just with application, substitution, and variation.

To use the preposition, one must have two or more elements. These elements may have different meanings, be similar, or may have some combination. Then, the application of the preposition either expresses the extant relationship of the elements or delineates what the relationships should or will be. Care should be taken in selecting the preposition to describe an existing condition, however there is a chance to explore and play with the introduction of a preposition to describe the interaction of the elements. To be capricious with the preposition allows a flexibility in spatial construction and it can create new relationships and designs that were never previously explored. Several references in popular and architectural culture use the switching related prepositions. The Beatles mention to be within you and without you. Wright describes a structure as being of the hill, not on the hill. These examples show that the replacement of the preposition can wholly change the meaning of a sentence or phrase. This is the way in which a simple substitution can completely change a form or spatial relationship.

In addition, the use of variation of prepositions encourages complexity in spatial forms and relationships. To use multiple prepositions to describe the interaction of elements adds nuance and complicated forms. For two walls to be *upon* and *about* may confuse or set off the imagination. For a person to be *above* and *amid* the trees, what does that mean? Can it mean anything? Can it mean multiple things? Yes. One does not have to accept the use of any combination of prepositions, but it is a good way to brainstorm and improvise when designing. Also, there are different types of meaning: one can be literal or figurative; one can be concrete or abstract. There are options for the designer. So, the architect can work with the preposition after defining the elements and possibly after determining the program, spaces, site, and materials. However, the architect can use this method even before these, especially if trying to explore the interplay of spaces and forms.

As a game, the designer can define the elements of play, choose a preposition or prepositions, and a verb or verbs, if desired. Within this set of words, relationships, and actions, there are many possibilities, and each possibility is different. Furthermore, if multiple prepositions are chosen, the designer can choose the order of operation, as well as the combination of operations, if desired. So, A then B can give a very different relationship than B then A. Again, A plus B can give even another relationship, different than the previous. Once you have more than two prepositions, there are many combinations and variations, and there are many ways to play and be successful at this little game.

Preposition Types

There are several different types of prepositions, and each of these can be used in the design and description of space. These prepositional types are: time, place, movement, manner, agent of instrument, measure, source, and possession.

Prepositions of Time

Prepositions of Time describe when something happened, relative to another word. Some of the most common examples of Prepositions of Time are: *before, after, during, at, in,* and *on.* In English, some of the prepositions can be multiple types, such as *at, in,* and *on.* These examples can also be Prepositions of Place. This can be confusing for non-native speakers, but it gives a great opportunity to explore the spatial possibilities when moving between the types.

Some might initially suggest that Prepositions of Time do not relate to space, but we can think of time as really the experience of changing space. With many projects, especially in school, the building or building elements are used to measure time, such as the shadows on a building, the natural ebb and flow of people and their use of space throughout the day, building systems, and lighting from dusk through night to dawn. However, another way one can look at the passage of time is to mark the passage through space or spaces. To come *before* a building entrance means both the position, but also the imminent entry which can be experienced through site and imagined through the mind. To express something *during* the experience of space describes the occasion of one action concurrent with another. To walk *through* a space while others walk past you, in the other direction, is an example of during. The interaction and speed of passing are experiences that occur during the users' actions.

A list of Prepositions of Time that are explored in this work include:

About

Across

After

Ahead Of

Along

Amid

Among

As

At

Before

Behind

Between

Beyond

By

Circa

Close To

During

Following

In

In Between

Inside

Near

Of

On

Outside Of

Over

Past

Pending

Prior To

Round

Till

To

Toward

Under

Until

Up To

Up Until

Upon

With

Within

Prepositions of Place

Prepositions of Place describe location, and this location can be of objects or the viewer. This is important to keep in mind, especially as design is about space for human use, and most of the best structures explore the possibilities of the human body in space. To think of a person *within* a structure is very different than thinking of the person walking *on* the floor –one describes space and interaction with it, while the other expresses traversing a two-dimensional surface that is passive. With this example, think about using another preposition, other than *on*. What happens when we walk *versus* the floor or when we walk *within* the floor? With this substitution, the imagination brings us to a new place where elements are not quite what we typically think of them. Why can't we be moving *versus* or *against* a floor? Why can't we walk *inside* the floor? What is a floor? We use the term floor to describe the building element, but also we use it to describe a story. Can the story, or level, act like a floor, work like a floor, or evoke the nature of floorness, while creating a spatial exploration that extends well beyond the flat plane?

Again, there are many Prepositions of Place and these prepositions express spatial relationships. This type of preposition may be the nearest and dearest to the architect, and there are many examples of this type of preposition. However, do not forget about the other types of prepositions to add even more depth to a space or place.

Here are the Prepositions of Place explored in this work:

Aboard

About

Above

Across

Against

Along

Along With

Alongside

Amid

Amidst

Among

Amongst

Apart From

Around

Astride

At

Atop

Away From

Before

Behind

Below

Beneath

Beside

Besides

Between

Beyond

By

Circa

Close To

Cum

Down

Following

Forward Of

From

In

In Between

In Front Of

In Lieu Of

In The Face Of

In View Of

Including

Inside

Into

Near

Near To

Of

Off

On

On Board

On Top Of

Onto

Opposite

Opposite To

Out Of

Outside

Outside Of

Over

Past

Round

Through

Throughout

To

Together With

Touching

Toward

Under

Underneath

Up

Up Against

Up To

Upon

Versus

Via

Vis-à-Vis

With

Within

Without

It is important to remember that one can use multiple prepositions, not just one. Next, we will look at Prepositions of Movement, which is like change of place over time.

Prepositions of Movement

Another type of preposition is a Preposition of Movement. This is the change in position over time, so there are overlaps between this type of preposition and the previous two. In any case, some examples include *to, across, from,* and *round*, and these describe motion. Most buildings try to avoid motion which would show structural failure or at least dynamics. However, a figurative motion can apply to most buildings and building elements, and literal movement can describe the building users, HVAC, plumbing, and the electrical system, or maybe there are parts of a structure that actually move. Modernism expressed structures as practical machines or instruments where there was a great deal of dynamism for the elements within or outside the walls, but the structure would steadfastly hold its form throughout time. In this way, the building becomes a canvas or baseline, which reflects the changes around and inside it.

Moving beyond the Modern, why couldn't a structure move and change? What other built structures are in motion? Boats, trucks, and trailers can be inhabited, and they have moving parts. Could a portion of a roof detach from a structure on moderate spring and fall days? Can a building's face turn to the sun or wind? These questions expand the boundaries of a structure's design. Maybe a building can move, or maybe it is just the constituent parts that move –this is up to the designer using the Prepositions of Movement where another preposition might have been used. What happens when we replace one preposition with another? To have a wall that moves *from* a floor –what does that mean? Is this wall like a large overhead door? Is it on hinges or slides that make it fly from the ground? Or, is it just a figure of speech?

These are the Prepositions of Movement represented in this work:

About

Across

Around

Away From

Beside

Beyond

By

Circa

Close To

Down

For

From

Further To

Near To

Next To

Onto

Out Of

Outside Of

Over

Past

Round

Throughout

To

Toward

Under

Underneath

Up

Up To

Via

Prepositions of Manner

Prepositions of Manner are terms that express how something could or does happen. An element within the building may be only that element, but it is possible for it to transform or translate as or with something else. A few Prepositions of Manner are: *like, by,* and *with*, and each of this type of preposition provides a change through conveyance. A ceiling that moves *by* air pressure creates a changing form through the variation of air flow, and a foundation that moves *by* hydraulic pressure uses water to create dynamism. So, this form of preposition relies on the object of the preposition to alter the verb and subject, transferring the ability through the use of the Preposition of Manner.

What happens when we substitute another preposition type with a Preposition of Manner? A building standing *on* the water has a different sense than a building standing *like* the water or a building standing *with* the water, and what about a building standing *by* the water? Not the proximity to water, but structural integrity through the use of the water. The nature of the objects changes dramatically just with altering one word. Another example could be a stair *near* a light. What is a stair *like* a light? How do you imagine a stair *in* a light? The stair is elevated to another, different object, and it creates a point of interest. Words can be used to facilitate or guide the transformation of objects through a translation from form to words and manipulating these words. Then, when the wordplay is complete, one can resurrect the object, though in a changed and other way.

Here are Prepositions of Manner
that are explored in this work:

À La

After

As Per

Because Of

But For

By

By Means Of

Depending On

Due To

For

Given

In

Less

Like

On

On Board

On Top Of

Out Of

Owing To

Per

Re

Regarding

Through

To

Together With

Upon

Via

With

Next, we will look at Prepositions of Agent or Instrument, which is somewhat similar to Prepositions of Manner, as well as Prepositions of Measure, which are used to explain the amount or greatness of a thing or things.

Prepositions of Agent

Prepositions of Agent show something completed or acted through someone or some other thing. This type of preposition describes the author and the realm of the object, and it explains the means of the action or creation. These prepositions are shared with other preposition types, but the prepositions help describe the main object by the object of the preposition, as a modifier, similar to an adverb or adjective.

The Preposition of Agent can be used in design straight, as intended, or it can be substituted for another type, as shown before. The house *in* the field has a very different meaning to a house *by* the field. The latter shows the field is the author of the house. In this example, the house is no longer just an object in the landscape. Instead, it is an object that is designed by the field, sharing the same materials, geometries, and essence of the field. Architects that are interested in the spirit of the place would love the house *by* the field. How did the field make the house? The structure uses the stones from the field, as well as the constituent grasses and earth of the field. How is the structure similar to the field? The house is flat with small undulations to shed water from its roof, mimicking the land and its surroundings.

Some might ask why the field would make the house, and so it is important to understand the meaning and purpose of the field and the house. The field is there to grow crops or feed animals, and it has been chosen for this by its characteristics and qualities. Some places, like a beach or mountain, are not good for growing plants or sustaining livestock: it is not in their nature, they do something else. Why is the house on the site? To support the individuals working the land to provide the food source. So, it makes sense that the land might design the house. Of course, the land is not a human, so there are liberties, but using the Preposition of Agent not only helps with the understanding of the nature of the house, but also pushes the designer to be especially conscious of how the building matches or works with the site.

Prepositions of Agent used in this work are:

About

By

From

With

Prepositions of Measure

Prepositions of Measure describe how the quantity of something is determined. The structure might be determined by the number of 2×4s, and this would mean something different than a structure by the square foot. The choice of the measurement describes the quality of the object. Someone who is asking about a house and its 2x4s really cares about the structure of the house, but especially about how it is constructed with 2x4s. Whereas, a house by the square foot implies that the viewer or user is desirous of a structure with a large or small area, based on the square footage. There are many ways to measure something, even if the method of measurement is figurative or abstract. A room that is measured by hopes and dreams suggests a space that is important for the production and imagination of ideas and how to implement them.

The use of this type of preposition in design can be with substitution with another type or by manipulating the objects in the phrase. Choosing the measurement units means so much in this type, where the choice of unit determines how the object is viewed. In this way, meaning is in the eye of the beholder, and it is necessary that the one appraising understand the composition and characteristics of the work for the meaning to make sense. One might try to measure a room in pancakes, but if the architect never thought about pancakes in the composition of the space, the imposed meaning is silly. However, it is possible to post-rationalize something or even someone using a lens from a different space or time. If the object exists in the new or extended space or time, then it might be allowable to use this method of judgement. However, if the one critiquing the structure or space is using characteristics or conditions that are alien to the building or place, then the ideas should not be admissible. Authorship is a form of ownership, and meaning is shared between the two.

Prepositions of Measure in this work include:

By

Of

With

We will look at Prepositions of Source, giving the origins of objects through the use of the preposition, and we will discuss the Preposition of Possession, which gives authorship or ownership through the preposition or prepositional phrase. You will find that there are overlaps among the types.

Prepositions of Source

Prepositions of Source show from where something or someone came. This preposition type describes the main object by its origin. The nature of the object is tethered to the other, although it or the viewer may not understand or define it through this relationship. However, when the elements are framed by the Preposition of Source in the sentence or phrase, the relationship is clear. This preposition type serves as a modifier, and it is immutable. Unlike previous examples, this relationship is real, not figurative, so the genealogy is clear, and the relationship is absolute.

To use the Preposition of Source in design, we use the type to define origin, and the essence or signature of the progenitor is intrinsic in the following entity. We can underline this source to ensure the nature of both is carried forward, and it is not possible for the relationship to be false. Otherwise, we can once again play a game of substitution. We can use the Preposition of Source in place of any other type, as long as the object is not strictly defined. For example, one can say the windows are *along* the wall. By changing the type to preposition of source, we can get the windows are *from* the wall. This provides an understanding that the geometry of the wall allows for windows that perhaps fold out to allow both light and protection from the weather. In this case, the designer must ask what the wall is made of to have windows spring forth. Maybe, the wall is made of glass and sectioned or mullioned: these sections might fold like paper to provide apertures. Or, the wall might be clapboard, though it is partitioned and the window is simply one of the partitioned sections that is seemingly excised or cut and folded to provide the opening. In both options, the wall provides the window, but the window helps divide the wall. Is it possible for this to be the case in other examples of prepositions of source? If we receive energy *from* the sun, then the energy is *of* the sun, but the sun is the energy source. Although it is not reflexive, there is a balanced understanding that one is the same or nearly the same as the other. This example allows the understanding of the sun as energy, and energy as that which comes from the sun.

Prepositions of Source used in this work include:

By

From

Of

Prepositions of Possession

The final preposition type is the Preposition of Possession. The Preposition of Possession marks something that is owned by someone or something. This ownership defines the item, but it can also define the owner. The furniture *of* the woman is understood to be the woman's, but the woman is also now understood to be someone who has furniture. That can be important, especially to someone who might not have or would like to give furniture. Furthermore, the furniture is not some random grouping, it is the furniture of the woman, placed as the woman prefers. In this way, both are defined and connected.

How can we use the Preposition of Possession in design. To know that something controls or owns something else describes both that object and the relationship of the two, where one controls the other. There is a major and a minor, and the relationship cannot be flipped, except as a figurative play. The walls *of* the building are the building's walls, however these walls define the building, as well. The structure would not be the same without the presence of these walls. Of course, the walls in the structure belong only to that structure, but can we look at the design and makeup of the structure as a series of walls? How is this different than a grouping of spaces or the limits of the foundation and site? Can the designer pull out the wallness of the building. What makes a building wally, and what does this give the user? Is there something superior in this nature to that of a normative building? What do walls give us that other elements don't? In another example, the steps *of* a stair are the stair's steps, but the stair is not a stair without steps and so one allows the other. But, there is a hierarchy: the stairs own or control the steps. Steps without stairs are flooring. Stairs without steps are still stairs, though they are not easy to ascend. Can something be made of this hierarchy? This and substitution allow the designer to explore new relationships in architecture.

Prepositions of Possession included in this work include:

Of

To

With

Let's Play the Preposition Game I

Here is one example of how to use prepositions to create or affect a design. What surprises will we come up with as the game unfolds?

1. Introduction of phrase.

For this first example, let's start with an overall structure and let it relate to the landscape in some way. For the program, we will use an art center, and it will be in the piedmont of the Appalachian mountains. To start, the phrase is:

The art center is near a rock outcropping and waterfall.

This is a nice location for an art center, but how is the center sited relative to the land features? Another Preposition of Place would be helpful, and we might want to add a secondary preposition type –let's see.

2. Examination of preposition use.

The art center is near a rock outcropping and waterfall.

To use *near* describes the proximity but nothing else. Is this *near, above*? *Near, under*? *Near, among*. A general description allows us to understand that the objects can be seen or visited in the location, but that is it. Are there any other shared characteristics or descriptions?

3. Analyze preposition use.

Should we change the preposition to improve the design? If we are designing a new art center that does not have the spatial relationships spelled out, then yes. Furthermore, if the art center already exists, then we should provide more specificity for a better description and writing. To be *near* something does not fully describe the relationship. Instead, we could use a more specific preposition, such as *inside, behind,* or *upon*. There are others that can provide a more abstract position, such as *till, of,* or *as*.

4. Develop existing or create new preposition use.

In this example, let's replace the existing preposition with the six example prepositions above:

The art center is inside a rock outcropping and waterfall.

The art center is behind a rock outcropping and waterfall.

The art center is upon a rock outcropping and waterfall.

The art center is till a rock outcropping and waterfall.

The art center is of a rock outcropping and waterfall.

The art center is as a rock outcropping and waterfall.

Let's look at each of these sentences:

The art center is inside a rock outcropping and waterfall.

In this possibility, the center is an interior, hidden by the landscape features. It is likely that the surfaces of the space are or reflect the outcropping and waterfall. Maybe the walls are rusticated with the stone of the outcropping creating a mottled, undulating surface. Maybe the waterfall is like a window or sculpture–something with visual interest.

The art center is behind a rock outcropping and waterfall.

This possibility could be the art space hiding in the land, divorced from the outcropping and the waterfall. This design choice allows each object to have its own definition, and although they are nearby, they do not need to interrelate or communicate. This sentence allows each to have its own program and needs.

The art center is upon a rock outcropping and waterfall.

The use of upon makes the art center heroic, above the outcropping and waterfall. In this relationship, the rock and cascade serve and support the art center, and the space is enriched by the landscape. The center does not necessarily change the understanding of the outcropping and waterfall, but it can affect them.

The art center is till a rock outcropping and waterfall.

This is maybe a strange relationship, but we can understand it as a separation between the natural and the human. The art center exists up to the rock and water, where there is a break, and all of the objects are able to exist independently. In some ways, this is similar to the behind example, but there is an adjoining condition where one abuts the other.

The art center is of a rock outcropping and waterfall.

The use of the preposition *of* tells us that the outcropping and waterfall are materials or resources for the creation of the art center. In this way, the stone will act as stone to define the center, and the water will flow like water, creating spaces that blend very well with their context. This is a fine selection for developing the spirit of the place.

The art center is as a rock outcropping and waterfall.

As is similar to *of*, but the difference is that this relationship infers the art center is a simulation of the landscape features or parts of them. The materials may act the same, but they do not need to be the same. Concrete can act like stone, and fabric can act like water. The center complements the outcropping and waterfall.

5. Evaluate the preposition use.

Most architects would likely go to the choice of *of* for this example –it allows the most for the design. However, the use of *till* creates a complicated and novel option.

Let's Play the Preposition Game II

1. Introduction of phrase.

In this example, we will look at a smaller scale design –a seat that is in context with a wall. The additional details are not accounted for, because we can use the preposition to define the detailing. The starting phrase is:

The seat is at the wall.

This relationship could be very mundane. But, what if it is not? Again, more specificity will be very helpful to determine the relationship, and another preposition could do the trick. Otherwise, what is the meaning of *at*? Is it more than a general location marker, giving proximity to something else? Is there a interrelation of the object and the place?

2. Examination of preposition use.

To be *at* something explains the location relative to another object, but it also filters the extent of location. To be *at* something implies that one is present but not part of the place. The entity that is *at* is *near* and *around*, but not *of*– there is alienation and separateness in the condition of being *at* someplace. How close of a relationship is *at*?

3. Analyze preposition use.

Beyond the preposition and its relationship, we need to know more about the seat, and we might define the wall with the seat, or it could be the other way around. We can use a Preposition of Place, but it could also be possible to use Prepositions of Manner, Movement, or Possession. We will experiment with three variations of two types.

First, we look at Prepositions of Movement, and we will use the prepositions: *across, down*, and *out of*.

Second, we will use Prepositions of Manner, such as *because of, given*, and *together with*.

4. Develop existing or create new preposition use.

We will replace the preposition in this exercise.

The seat is at the wall can change to:

The seat is across the wall.

The seat is down the wall.

The seat is out of the wall.

The seat is because of the wall.

The seat is given the wall.

The seat is together with the wall.

Now, let's review each sentence.

These sentences use Prepositions of Movement:

The seat is across the wall.

In this example, the seat extends the length of the wall. Perhaps, this wall is in the shape of a bench allowing all to sit–an egalitarian choice. Another possibility is a single seat that extends the length of the wall –in this case, it is either a short wall or a big seat. What would come of a big seat? Is it purely theatrical? Is there some scalar game that makes the user either appear big or small, depending on the application?

The seat is down the wall.

This possibility implies that there is one lonely seat at an end or bottom of a wall. The wall could be any size, but it seems large and imposing, driving the individual in the seat to loneliness and separation. Who would sit in this seat? Why would they want to sit in the seat? This seat might be for someone who is antisocial or oppressed.

The seat is out of the wall.

Here, the seat springs forth from the wall. An impression of or opening for the chair is behind, and it seems the seat and the wall will not be recombined. There might be some relief that the two are irreconcilable from the advantage of the seat. Space separates the objects and is charged with the action of this change.

These examples use Prepositions of Manner:

The seat is because of the wall.

In this example, the seat does not exist without the wall. The wall virtually makes the seat. Its importance requires a seat to think about or act on the occasion of the wall. What drives the wall or its context to create the seat? Otherwise, is the seat part of the wall? Can the seat exist without the wall?

The seat is given the wall.

This option is similar to the previous. In essence, the wall causes the seat, and both are considered in relation to one another. In what situation is this useful? What is the purpose of the wall? And, the purpose of the seat? What does one give the other?

The seat is together with the wall.

Although we could argue this preposition choice is similar to the previous two, in actuality the seat and wall are separate from one another, even though they share the same space. There might be similarities between the seat and the wall, but this is not necessary.

5. Evaluate the preposition use.

The Prepositions of Manner are more abstract, and in this case, they are arguably better. Of the three, the one that stands out with the most opportunity is:

The seat is because of the wall.

This is an interesting sentence with several possible resulting designs.

Let's Play the Preposition Game III

1. Introduction of phrase.

For the next example, let's zoom out and look at the urban scale. Architects need to look at buildings and their context at multiple levels to draw meaning and connection, and the use and choice of prepositions can help this process. Again, we will use simple terms for the objects as we explore this game. Let's use structure and city as the words.

The structure is within the city.

Within is a Preposition of Place, and it defines the location of the building rather well. However, the preposition doesn't explain the relationship of the building to the city, other than being amongst the constituent buildings and streets of the city. Can we further define the condition of the building relative to the city? What makes this structure and its location in the city important?

2. Examination of preposition use.

To be *within* requires other elements that are likely similar, however they may have quite a bit of variation. What is important is the conglomeration of the various elements creates an interior where the main subject sits. The term is composed of *with-* and *-in*; *with* informs us that the elements are a group, creating an aggregation, whereas *in* describes the location relative to the others of the group.

3. Analyze preposition use.

We understand that the structure is *within* the city, but can we have a better description of how the building works *with* the urban environment and the urban environment works *with* the building? The description in the given statement provides a Preposition of Place; although we could use another of this type, we can explore other relationships using one of the other preposition types. In this exercise, we will use Prepositions of Manner and Agent.

For Prepositions of Manner, we will look at the prepositions *after, depending on*, and *regarding*.

As for the Prepositions of Agent, we will use *about, by*, and *from*. There are similarities between Prepositions of Manner and Agent, but we will try to have difference in the options.

4. Develop existing or create new preposition use.

Once again, we will replace the preposition in the initial sentence.

The structure is within the city becomes:

The structure is after the city.

The structure is depending on the city.

The structure is regarding the city.

The structure is about the city.

The structure is by the city.

The structure is from the city.

Now, let's review each sentence:

The following sentences use Prepositions of Manner.

The structure is after the city.

The use of *after* tells us that relative to the structure, the city is primary. Later in this experiment we will see other, similar descriptions that are like another definition of *after*, but even that definition requires the city to be first and the structure second. Does the building follow and learn from the urban environment? Yes, this is very likely, but the building also must cede importance to the city in this example. The structure is not the object, the city is.

The structure is depending on the city.

Once again, the structure is second to the city, but it is very clear in this example that the city nourishes or supports the structure. The structure cannot exist without the city, which explains the nature of the structure, something of a wallpaper building that relies on the armature of the urban condition–outside of the city, the building would fail.

The structure is regarding the city.

This option anthropomorphizes the building, and it is actively watching and evaluating the city. The structure likely changes because of the conditions of the city, continuously transforming in reaction to what happens in the urban context. This is an exciting relationship that truly activates the structure–it is not just a passive object in the space.

These sentences use Prepositions of Agent:

The structure is about the city.

In this example, as alluded to above, the city defines the structure. Although the structure's nature is slightly different and perhaps less than the city, the building's description is composed of elements from the city. In this relationship, the city is primary and the structure is secondary, but the structure is like a mirror, reflecting the city's essence.

The structure is by the city.

This is another, similar example, but in this case, the city makes the structure, however the structure's nature can be different than the city's. How can this occur? How can a building be from an urban location but not be similar to that place? Usually, we would like the structure to relate to the city, but maybe the structure is responding to some inconsistency or deficit in the city.

The structure is from the city.

Here is another example of the building being born of the city. However, this choice of preposition is more general than other options. There is nothing wrong with the relationship of the structure to the urban environment, but this example has as much or perhaps less specificity than the original sentence, *the structure is within the city*.

5. Evaluate the preposition use.

From this example, the most interesting relationship found from the given prepositions is:

The structure is regarding the city.

This may be abstract, and it does not provide the exact meaning of the structure, but we understand that this building learns and reacts to the urban context. What does this mean? How can the architect make the building active, changing with the conditions?

Let's Play the Preposition Game IV

1. Introduction of phrase.

In the final example of the preposition game, let's zoom back in to something relatively small–an architectural detail. In this way, we will have looked at the various scales most architects use on their projects. For the detail, we will look at a door and how it connects to the wall–the jamb and its hinges. The phrase we will use is:

The hinge is fastened to the door.

The preposition type for *to* is Preposition of Movement. *To* describes the participle fastened and expresses the direction of the action. We gain minimal information about the hinge and its connection, because we understand a hinge as an articulated joint for a door–rarely do we discuss hinges in other ways. Certainly, hinges can be used for other purposes, but this example explores the hinge and the door.

2. Examination of preposition use.

To describes the general direction of the action. Its use expresses the imminent connection of two or more elements, and this connection creates a new understanding of the disparate parts coming together to create a new assembly, a new essence to the conjoined objects. This connection and new meaning is common in design and is one of the most rewarding parts of architecture–building is the joining of elements to create a new purpose or meaning.

3. Analyze preposition use.

We know that hinge becomes part of the door assembly by using the preposition *to*. But, the way it joins the door is not clear. Does the hinge connect to the face of the door? Does it attach at the corners of the door or inside the door to create a hidden connection? The choice of preposition can help define this interface. We want to know the location of the connection, and we want to understand how the door is changed or affected by the hinge and its integration. Let's look at the door and hinge exploring Prepositions of Manner and Place.

For Prepositions of Manner, we will try: *less, out of*, and *with*.

For Prepositions of Place, we will use: *above, around*, and *through*.

4. Develop existing or create new preposition use.

As before, we replace the original preposition with the alternates given above.

The hinge is fastened to the door changes to:

The hinge is fastened less the door.

The hinge is fastened out of the door.

The hinge is fastened with the door.

The hinge is fastened above the door.

The hinge is fastened around the door.

The hinge is fastened through the door.

These sentences use Prepositions of Manner:

The hinge is fastened less the door.

This is an awkward phrase, but it does have meaning. In this, we find that the hinge is important and the door is minor. In fact, the door may not have as much importance because of the hinge. What does this mean? The hinge could be the door, and the normative door is cast aside for the structure of the hinge acting as the door.

The hinge is fastened out of the door.

This preposition choice can have a couple meanings, but we will assume that the hinge is constructed from the door itself. Is the door composed of flexible, durable materials that can allow the door to rotate and open, when developed? Can the hinge be cut in the door?

The hinge is fastened with the door.

In this sentence, the hinge is described as fully integrated with the door. Although the two objects may be distinct, the detailing and connections make the hinge and the door fully incorporated, making a seamless connection and a solid whole. What are the materials of the door and the hinge? They do not need to be the same, but how do we make such integration?

These sentences use Prepositions of Place:

The hinge is fastened above the door.

This preposition clearly defines the relationship of the hinge and the door. The door appears to float free with the hinge above the door, disconnected. The hinge is to be forgotten and will be minimal to evade scrutiny, whereas the door absorbs the attention and detail.

The hinge is fastened around the door.

Around ensures the hinge will not be forgotten. In fact, the hinge takes center stage and controls the door. Detailing for the hinge pulls the eye from the door, which is likely simple and not of note. However, the door must have substance, solid and capable of work.

The hinge is fastened through the door.

This phrase shows the hinge as integrated with the door, but the interconnection of the two requires the door to be altered to allow the mechanical attachment of the hinge to the door. This could be beautiful with fine detailing. The hinge may be nearly invisible with its form partially within the door.

5. Evaluate the preposition use.

There are several good options from the six preposition substitutions, but the chosen sentence is:

The hinge is fastened out of the door.

There are many questions with this example, and these questions can create very interesting details and material choices. In fact, the phrase could push the very definition of a door, if taken a certain way. This sentence can lead to several good designs.

Preposition Definitions

In this section, we will review most of the prepositions in contemporary English, which has more prepositions than any other language. Some prepositions have been removed because of similarity, such as *amongst* versus *among*, however the designer has nearly complete access to the ideas and possibilities of spatial relationships expressed in the language. Each preposition is provided alphabetically for ease of reference, and the definition for each is provided in three different forms: a line diagram, a spatial isometric, and a verbal description.

At the top of each preposition page, there is a line diagram. The line diagram is a rudimentary form expressing the relationship of elements through two-dimensional shapes, such as circles, lines, and rectangles. The constrained forms and linetypes provide legibility and continuity across the array of prepositions, and this format allows a simple understanding and abstraction which allows novel solutions and points of view.

In the middle of each page, there is a spatial isometric drawing. The spatial isometrics provide spatial relationships of the elements with the representation of form and dimensionality. In many instances, the isometrics are extrapolations of the line diagrams, but these drawings provide a simple architectural understanding without particular project specificity or detailing through elementary forms. Furthermore, these elementary, dimensional drawings allow accessible, objective descriptions of the spatial relationships.

Toward the bottom of each page, beneath the preposition title, there is a verbal description. In many ways, this description is close to a traditional dictionary definition, however the verbal description provides an interpretation and a rudimentary analysis of its use and nature to promote the best implementation of the preposition to express a spatial relationship. For the designer, this form of description is arguably more subjective, but the abstraction of the written word allows the synthesis of more creative design solutions through playful interpretation.

As a whole, the group of prepositions demonstrates the great number of spatial opportunities and variations. The simplified forms of the descriptions for the prepositions allow them to be applied to various contexts and scales. So, the use of a preposition can produce a particular detail, spatial structure, or section of a city.

It is encouraged that the designer review the prepositions in relation to the previous and following sections of this book. With an enriched understanding of each preposition, the designer will have stronger implementations in the preposition game and a greater knowledge of meaning in the examples given.

A bunny went à la the log.
A bunny went aboard the log.
A bunny went about the log.
A bunny went above the log.
A bunny went according to the log.
A bunny went across the log.
A bunny went after the log.
A bunny went against the log.
A bunny went ahead of the log.
A bunny went along the log.
A bunny went along with the log.
A bunny went alongside the log.
A bunny went amid the log.
A bunny went amidst the log.
A bunny went among the log.
A bunny went amongst the log.
A bunny went anti the log.
A bunny went apart from the log.
A bunny went around the log.
A bunny went as the log.
A bunny went as for the log.
A bunny went as per the log.
A bunny went as to the log.
A bunny went as well as the log.
A bunny went aside from the log.
A bunny went astride the log.
A bunny went at the log.
A bunny went atop the log.
A bunny went away from the log.
A bunny went bar the log.
A bunny went barring the log.
A bunny went because of the log.
A bunny went before the log.
A bunny went behind the log.
A bunny went below the log.
A bunny went beneath the log.
A bunny went beside the log.
A bunny went besides the log.
A bunny went between the log.

A bunny went beyond the log.
A bunny went but the log.
A bunny went but for the log.
A bunny went by the log.
A bunny went by means of the log.
A bunny went circa the log.
A bunny went close to the log.
A bunny went concerning the log.
A bunny went considering the log.
A bunny went contrary to the log.
A bunny went cum the log.
A bunny went depending on the log.
A bunny went despite the log.
A bunny went down the log.
A bunny went due to the log.
A bunny went during the log.
A bunny went except the log.
A bunny went except for the log.
A bunny went excepting the log.
A bunny went excluding the log.
A bunny went following the log.
A bunny went for the log.
A bunny went forward of the log.
A bunny went from the log.
A bunny went further to the log.
A bunny went given the log.
A bunny went gone the log.
A bunny went in the log.
A bunny went in addition to the log.
A bunny went in between the log.
A bunny went in case of the log.
A bunny went in favor of the log.
A bunny went in front of the log.
A bunny went in lieu of the log.
A bunny went in spite of the log.
A bunny went in the face of the log.
A bunny went in view of the log.
A bunny went including the log.
A bunny went inside the log.

à la

To reference or imitate another entity in order to define the subject. This relationship transforms one to another, whether literally or figuratively. Without the reference or copy, a clear description would not be possible without resorting to another method.

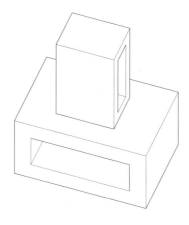

aboard

To exist on or within an object which is moving through a medium. The element in this state can be foreign to the object but both go to the same place.

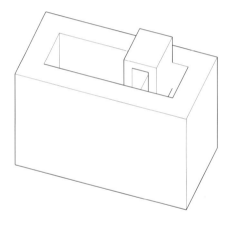

about

To reference, surround, or exist near another entity. The proximity acknowledges a connection or similarity between the two while accepting both are not exactly the same. The comparison allows one to nearly define another.

above

To be over or on top of another. Although this is common among objects or people, points of view and time can be defined with this vertical separation or change.

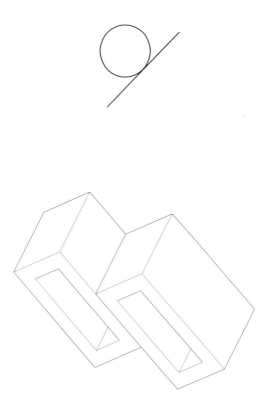

according to

To define a space or object by an authority or index. Placing a framework or structure over the entity provides a level of description that is verified relative to another position or time. The space or object in focus exists outside of this definition, but the addition of this provides an understanding from the other position.

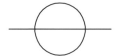

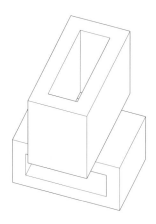

across

To span, move, or extend over a space, connecting or communicating from one point to another. The connection of the two spaces or times creates a third condition, which is that of joining, and the points can be compared or contrasted.

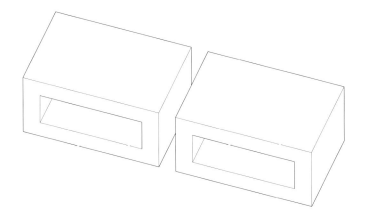

after

To exist or develop following some other object or time, but the previous object or time helps form or direct those that follow. An inevitable comparison comes from following another, however the subsequent entity can be wholly different than that before.

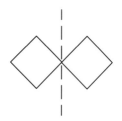

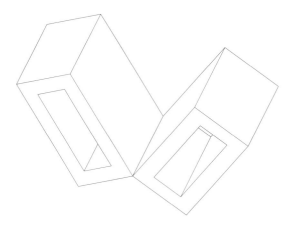

against

To be supported by or opposed to another entity. Neither is defined by the other, but a condition is developed in this relationship, and without one or the other, it is impossible to be in this position.

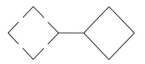

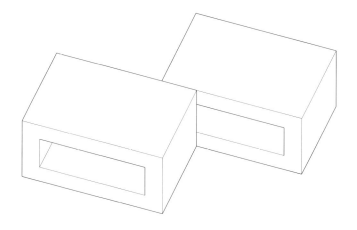

ahead of

To place before another in time or space. This positioning provides some advantage and describes a difference between the elements in sequence. The following's internal description may be different than the external description provided by that placed before.

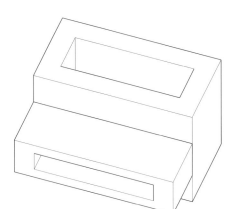

along

To extend or travel next to or with another entity or element. By moving in parallel, a similarity or connection is highlighted and creates a conglomeration or aggregation that is an expansion of the essence of the multiple individual parts.

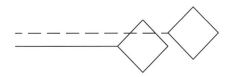

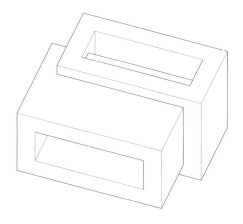

along with

To follow or proceed in the same direction. The condition implies a similarity and creates a group that helps define the constituent elements. In addition, the relationship implies directionality and a focal point.

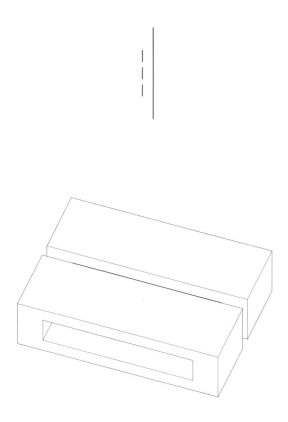

alongside

To exist or follow next to another or others. The proximity and similar course ensure the two or more entities are alike and promote comparison. The elements may be the same or considered the same.

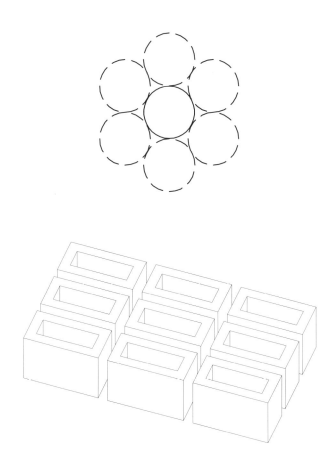

amid

To stand between two similar objects, states, or times. The entity exists in this liminal space partially or wholly defined by the surrounding condition.

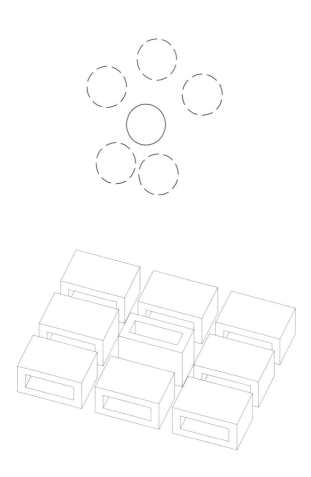

among

To exist around or within a set of elements where the nature of the group and the singular is defined by comparison and/or contrast. By being part of a group, that group's nature or characteristics are assumed to apply to the individual.

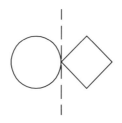

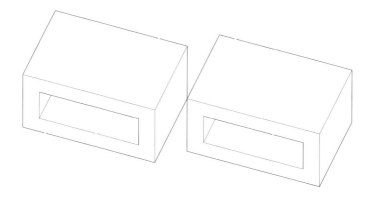

anti

To oppose an entity. The subject is different in nature and meaning to the other, and the relationship helps to define the characteristics of both elements being compared.

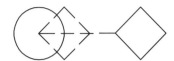

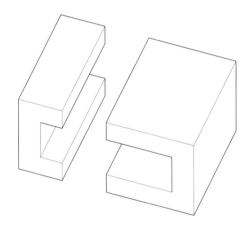

apart from

To stand or be outside or far from a limit or threshold that
defines a group. The separation ensures the element away
from the group or set is different, whether the difference
was inherent or brought by the removal of the object, space,
or time from the set.

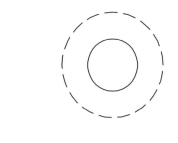

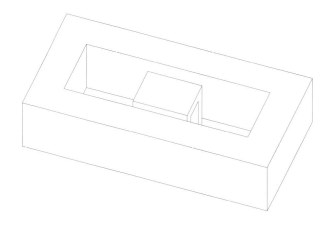

around

To circle or stand within a boundary, real or abstract, informed by a central point of focus. The center partially defines the object, space, or time that orbits. Movement is implied in the use of the term.

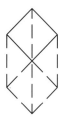

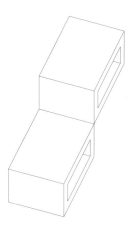

as

To act in the same manner or substitute for another.
The similarity between the two elements allows
interchangeability, however the two are not necessarily the
same. One may be a stand-in for the other with both having
different definitions.

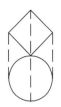

as for

To describe an element from a defined position both in relation to others and on its own. The point of view provides an understanding that may not be seen from the element itself. However, the description can help place a structure or order on the element.

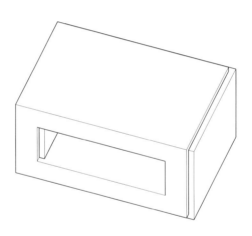

as per

To define an object, space, or time by an authority or index that is separate but has knowledge or understanding of the element. The definition of the one can be the same or slightly different than the description of itself by the object, space, or time.

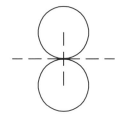

as to

To approximate or describe an object or time in relation to another. The two do not need to be related, instead they are two points connected by some commonality.

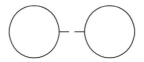

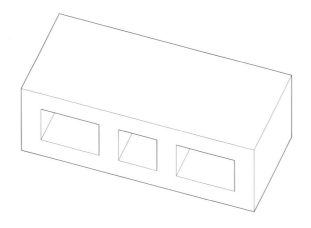

as well as

To add or include another or others to a group of similar elements. The relationship of these allows comparison of meaning and understanding. The additional element or elements may be minor to the group or others within the group.

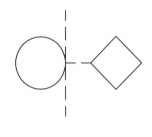

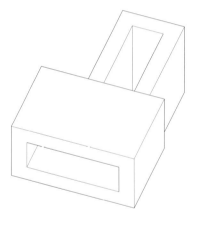

aside from

To define an entity by the exclusion or separation from another or others. The two might have similarities but will have differences that allow the classification or disconnection of the entities.

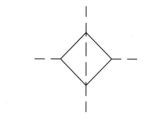

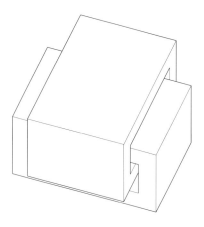

astride

To be on and probably straddling another. The subject is carried in the direction of the one beneath, and at least part of the understanding of this element is defined by the relationship and the destination.

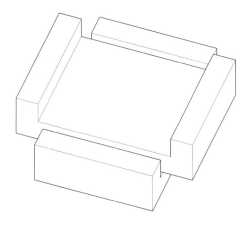

at

To be in the same time or space as another or others. The same period or location does not inherently mean the elements that share the same temporal or spatial point are the same or even similar. However, the shared allows comparison and definition through similarities.

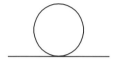

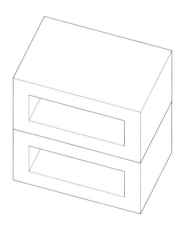

atop

To stand directly on and above an object. The condition provides an advantage to the element above and possible concealment for the object below. This position can be either temporary with entities in motion or permanent with inanimate objects.

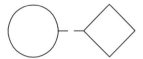

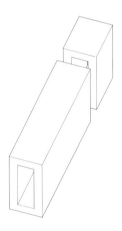

away from

To separate, either figuratively or literally. The parting of the two defines the relationship and also highlights the differences of those that separate. The elements may have similarities, but this is mostly a condition of contrast.

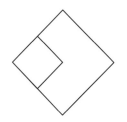

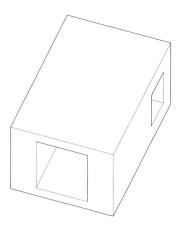

barring

To exclude and remove an entity from another condition where there is a complete and final separation of the two. This exclusion helps define the acting entity but not necessarily the one acted upon.

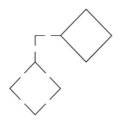

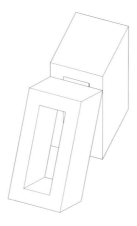

because of

To acknowledge the nature or understanding of an element by what proceeded or lead to the point of the element's existence. One creates or allows the creation of another, and both are described by the other's presence.

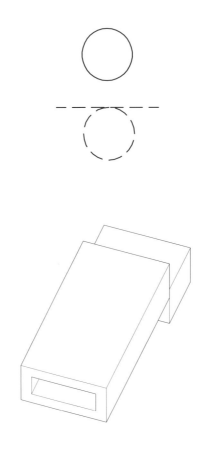

before

To place ahead in time or space. That placed in front of the other or others may be like those, however similarities are not required in this relationship. In fact, the separation of the elements defines a break or separation between the entities.

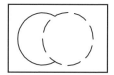

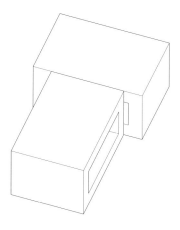

behind

To follow another in time or space. The spatial relationship is relative as the position of the viewer defines what comes before or follows, and this relationship allows both or all to affect one another.

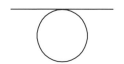

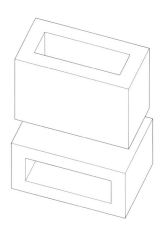

below

To describe the condition of being lower than another entity. This relationship can imply being lesser, protected, or supporting another, but the higher element is clearly either above or blanketing the other.

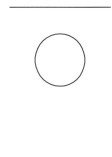

beneath

To exist below and under another, where the element above does not necessarily have an understanding or interest in that below. Both can be independent and different, but the element below must accept and acknowledge the presence of that above.

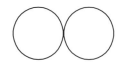

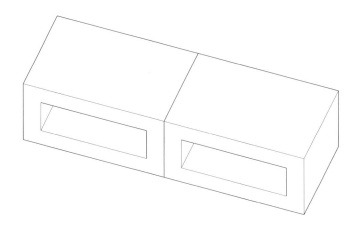

beside

To stand near and orient to another. This condition draws comparison and contrast, but marks these objects, times, or spaces as having similarities. In this way, the entities become a group, whether equal to or greater than the parts.

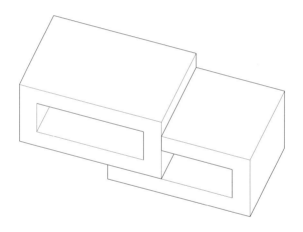

besides

To be next to or alongside another but not necessarily share a meaning or understanding. In this way, the elements in proximity do not have to be similar, but all in this relationship will share a definition of the whole.

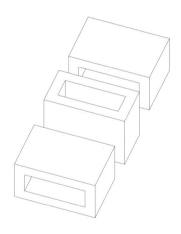

between

To stand within two other elements. The relationship draws a comparison of the three, however the elements do not have to be the same or similar. Nonetheless, the temporal or spatial relationship brings a meaning or definition to the group.

beyond

To exist outside a specific boundary. This state can be positive or negative, but the object or time is defined by the position outside of a set space or period.

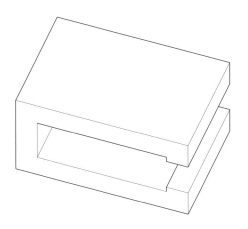

but

To exclude one from another. This exception partially
defines the one and allows a contrast to the other. This
condition can be positive but is often considered negative.

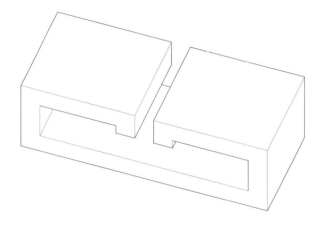

but for

To define another by a difference or addition. The
understanding of the element in focus cannot be given
without the understanding and acceptance of the other. So,
both must be presented allowing comparison and contrast.

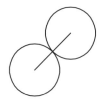

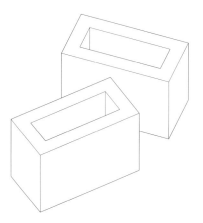

by

To be close to or created by another. A relationship between the two exists either through proximity or progenitor. The multiple definitions allow new plays on meaning.

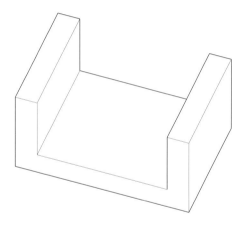

by means of

To mark the method or way something exists, moves, or changes. One is a catalyst or conveyance for the other to allow a translation or transformation in the nature and meaning of the element.

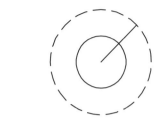

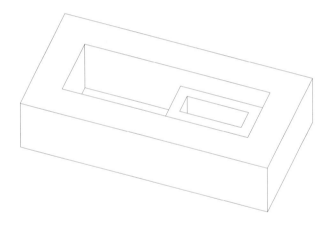

circa

To exist near some defined space, time, or limit. The entity is partially or wholly defined by this proximity, and this entity can affect or define the space, et cetera to a lesser extent.

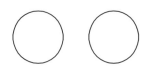

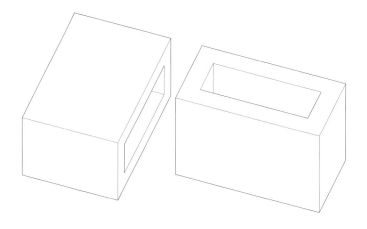

close to

To stand or be near another. The proximity expresses affinity or similarity between or among the elements nearby. The relationship draws comparisons while highlighting any apparent differences.

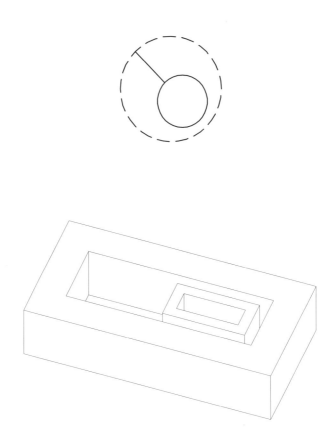

concerning

To bear meaning in relation to the observer or an object or time. There is a continuous, formal relationship between the two elements through a discrete or continuous space or time.

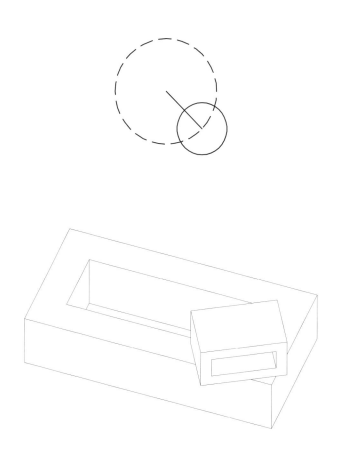

considering

To define through the comparison and contrast of one object or time to another or others. The view of one is subject to the other, so all are intertwined and affect one another.

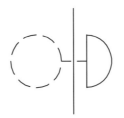

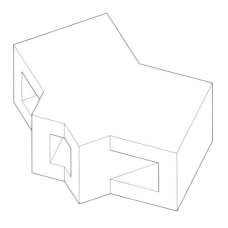

contrary to

To be against another physically or mentally and to
define both through their spatial or abstract relation. In
this condition, both or all elements are singular and well-
defined.

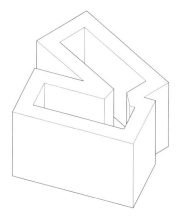

cum

To combine multiple elements to create a newly defined grouping or aggregation. The state or identity of the elements bears the meaning which transfers directly to the combination. This relationship is stronger than that of with.

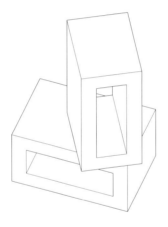

depending on

To rely on an object, action, or person, and one is ascendant to the other, creating a hierarchy. This condition or relationship draws comparison between the two entities, although they are not seen as equal.

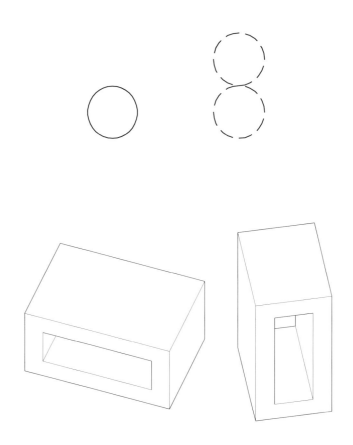

despite

To stand separate from another without any help or interaction between the entities. These contrast with one another to create a relationship of opposition or inconsequence.

down

To stand, place, or move an element lower relative to
another. The lower in this condition can be viewed as lesser
in some way to the higher object, space, or time. The term
defines position and can only exist in relation to another.

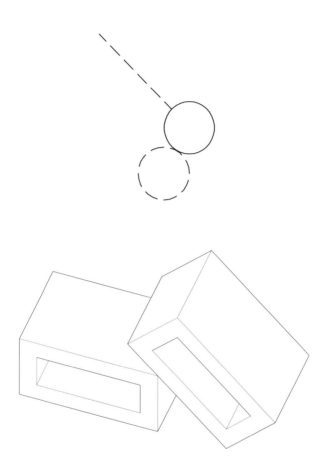

due to

To cause an event or moment that changes the direction or meaning of the following time or action. The two are tied in a conditional relationship where one describes or defines the other.

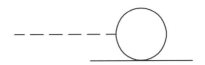

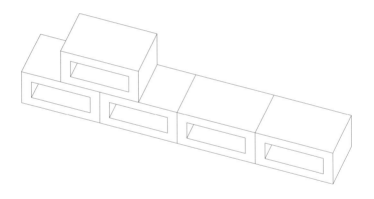

during

To exist at the same time as something else while working or being concurrent and separate from the other. The elements share a timeline, but do not have to share meaning.

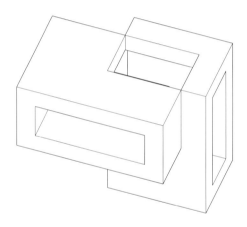

except

To define through the absence of a time, space, or object. The subtractive description defines the entity, but also provides or requires an understanding of the element or elements removed or not included.

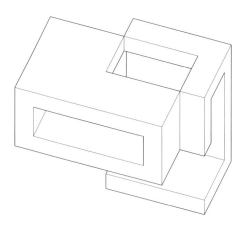

except for

To exclude one or some from a group or selection. This condition can be positive or negative and helps define those within and without through contrast.

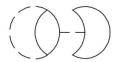

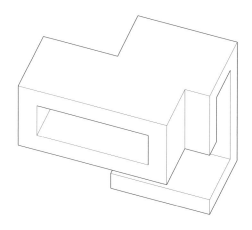

excepting

To exclude or deny another. This relationship defines the subject through the absence or separation of an element. This describes through opposition, instead of similarities.

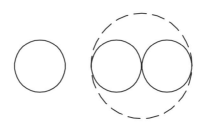

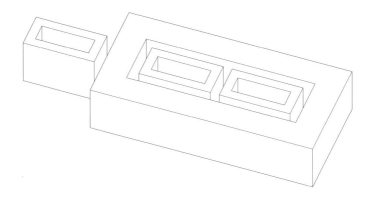

excluding

To separate from another. This separation is a characteristic of the entity where absence is presence, and the definition of the element must include the part removed.

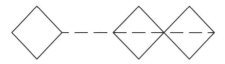

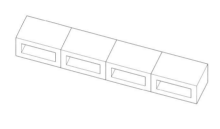

following

To be after another in time, space, or belief with or without a relationship between or among the entities. This condition is relative to a horological, physical, or mental position.

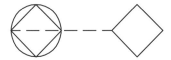

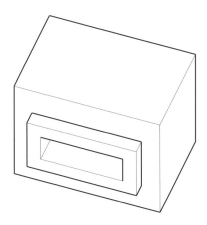

for

To describe something as having a purpose or requirement to another. The definition of the object is implied through the use of that object. With the entities separated, there is not a necessary relationship between them. However, when combined there is a similarity or purpose.

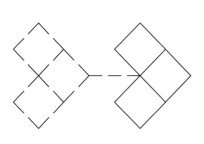

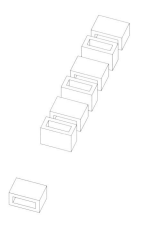

forward of

To be ahead of another or others, where the entities ahead are experienced before the others, whether in time or space. This relationship can provide a disadvantage to those that are behind, and there is not a necessary shared meaning or description.

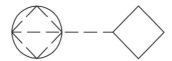

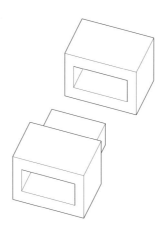

from

To come out of an entity or condition, which defines the one descending or extending out of the other, but may not define the home or source. However, the two are most often seen as similar to one another.

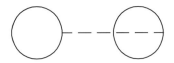

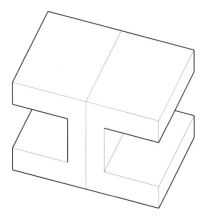

further to

To add to another, previous time or object, where the addition changes or improves the description of the other. The inclusion of the element changes the meaning of the entity added. The two are similar, but they reinforce each other.

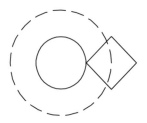

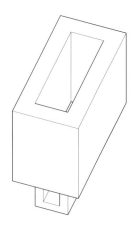

given

To pose relative to another viewpoint, object, or time. The relationship of the entities comes from the conditional circumstance of the two or more. What comes first defines what is next.

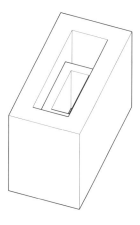

in

To be enclosed by spatial or temporal elements. This may or may not have or create a relationship between or among the related elements, however the condition easily defines another, at least in position.

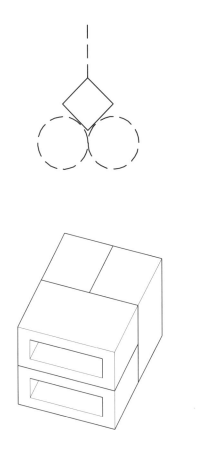

in addition to

To place an element with or above another or other elements to describe that entity as beyond or other than the elements it is grouped with. This provides a contrast first, and a comparison second.

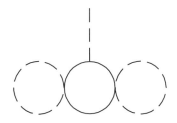

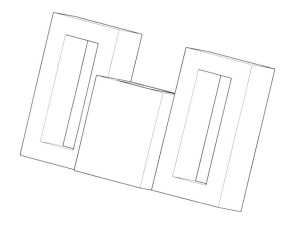

in between

To exist within the bounds of two entities. This relationship highlights the differences among the three, creating up to six conditions, although similarities may emerge from this state.

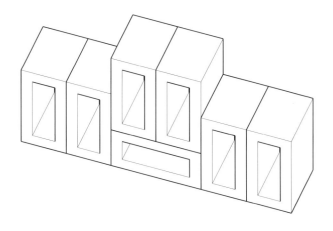

in case of

To use conditionally on the occurrence of an event or state, where one cannot exist or act without the presence of the other. In this way, the relationship and nature of the elements is only fully given at the incident.

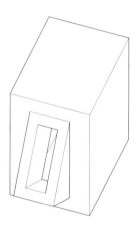

in favor of

To share a positive opinion of something or someone. The two can have similarities but the relationship helps describe the subject without definition of the one casting the opinion.

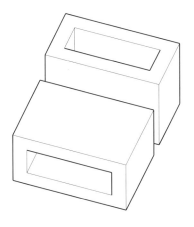

in front of

To stand or be ahead of others, most likely all facing
or progressing in the same direction. This relationship
describes the entity ahead as leading or directing the others.

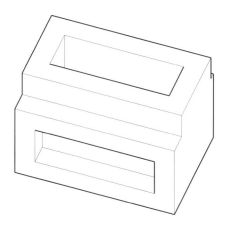

in lieu of

To replace or substitute an element for another in order to progress or function. This state defines a similarity between that absent and that present, and it questions the position of the element missing.

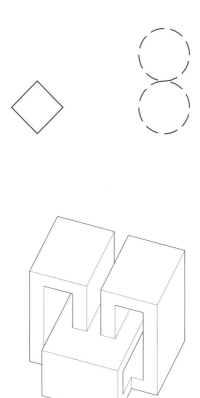

in spite of

To exist without or against the support or acknowledgement of another entity. This condition makes the subject opposed or outside the influence of someone or something.

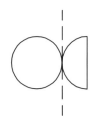

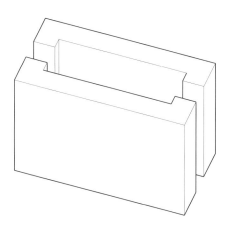

in the face of

To weigh an entity through the introduction of another. This creates a dynamic relationship where at least the subject transforms to evolve or cope with the other. The condition is either of comparison or contrast.

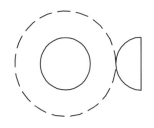

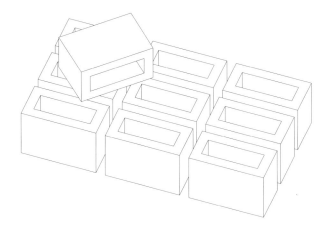

in view of

To define an element through the perspective of or by another. The two or more entities create relationships with one another through opposition, comparison, and contrast.

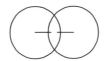

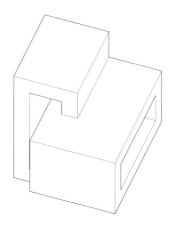

including

To describe by adding an entity or entities to a group. These additions give a better understanding of the whole or only an understanding of the initial element. There must be similarities between the entities in the group.

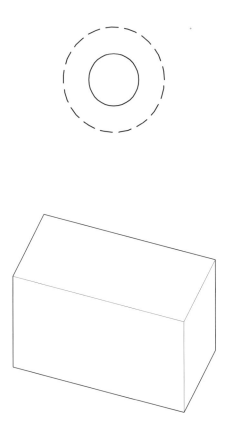

inside

To exist within a time, space, or enclosure and not extend beyond specific limits or boundaries. The element within does not need to be related to the envelope, but the container might operate as proxy for the contained.

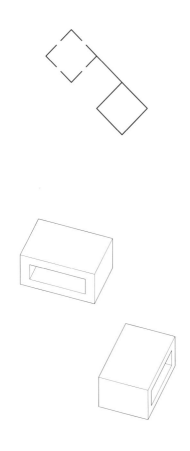

instead of

To use one in place of another as a substitute or improvement. The two must be similar or the same in that way that they can replace one another, however they might not be similar in any other way.

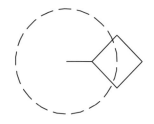

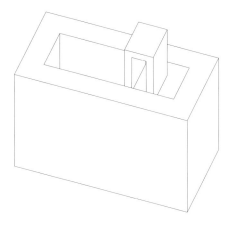

into

To enter within a defined physical or temporal boundary where that coming within is separate and not necessarily similar to the bounding condition. Understanding of the element entering changes with this.

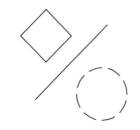

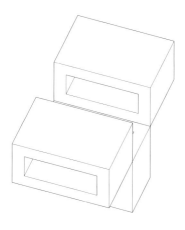

irrespective of

To be without the relationship to or acknowledgement of another where neither affects the other. As such the only relationship necessary is within the use or operation of the term.

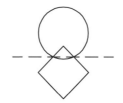

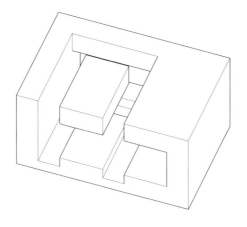

less

To explain the nature of an object, space, or time by the absence of another. This is a subtractive method of defining the condition, and the full understanding of the relationship can only occur with the description of that removed.

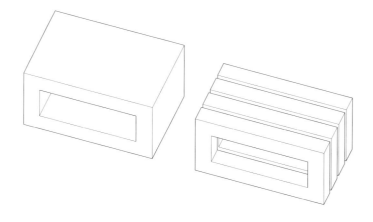

like

To exist or act in a manner similar to another. Both do not need to be the same, however they must have similarities that allow one to be or act like the other. In most cases, the elements truly are similar or nearly the same, and one might be able to interchange with another.

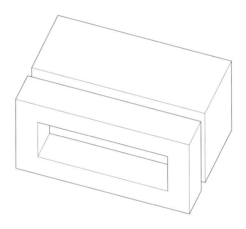

minus

To be without another or other. The lack of this or these provides a description and point of view of the element. The loss creates an irreparable change in the first.

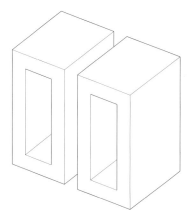

near

To be close to something or someone physically, mentally, or philosophically. The concrete or abstract proximity of two objects or people creates likeness and comparison, which helps to define both.

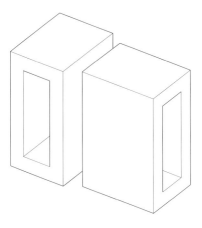

near to

To exist or be sympathetic to another, where there is
a similarity between the two, not just a relationship of
proximity. To define one is to define the other to some
extent in this juxtaposition.

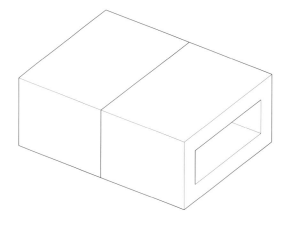

next to

To stand adjacent in time or space to another. The proximity creates commonality and definition of both, and without the similar location, there may not be a connection between the two.

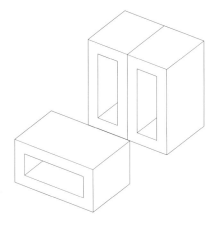

notwithstanding

To avoid the effect or nature of other elements and retain an understanding different than those being compared. The condition requires a contrast between the subject and the other elements.

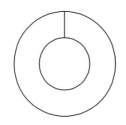

of

To stand in the spatial or temporal proximity of another and
to be part of a homogenous or similar aggregation. The
relationship is positive in the perspective of the surrounding
or similar.

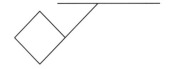

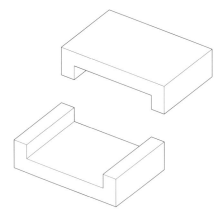

off

To produce or exist in a position where some element does not occur or stand in relation to a defined state. This can be the opposite of on an element or removed from the presence of the element.

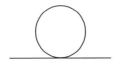

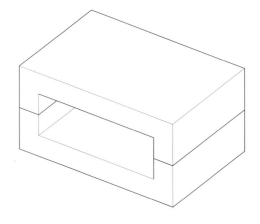

on

To stand and be supported by another element where the lower element is effectively a vehicle, foundation, or part for the entity above. Both describe each other.

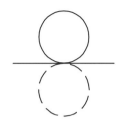

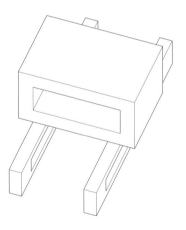

on account of

To create a state from the occurrence of some action or condition. The incident is the cause of the existence of the state, therefore the result is defined by the occurrence, but the action or condition is not described or reliant on the resultant state.

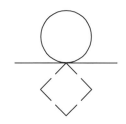

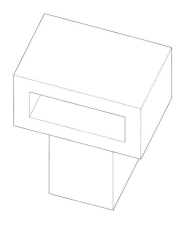

on behalf of

To act or stand in for another in order to meet some objective. The substitution is like a duplication of the original creating a virtual pair that share similarities.

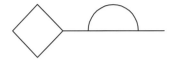

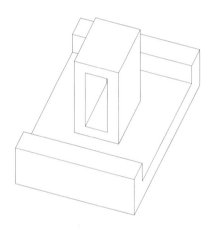

on board

To stand on or in an object with a defined level or plane
that is separated by elevation or composition from another
or other elements. This relationship implies inclusion and
connection.

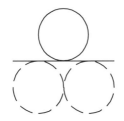

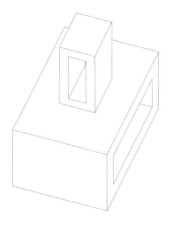

on top of

To exist with one entity resting or sitting over another. This can either define the element below to be inferior to or to be stronger than the element above. In addition, the higher entity can be described to be strengthened or improved by the lower.

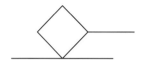

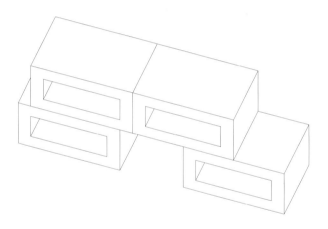

onto

To arrive upon an object for some advantage. Surmounting this, the environment or opportunity changes, providing a new vantage.

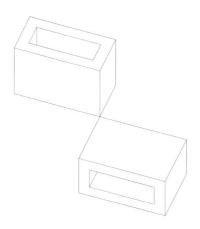

opposite

To stand and face another across a defined point or line. The entire relationship of the two is encapsulated in the position and orientation of both entities to create a specific condition.

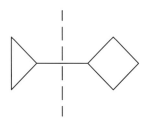

opposite to

To stand or space across, along some axis that is a position, focal point, or mirror line. The relationship of the two elements creates a third element between what is described by the confrontation of the initial two elements.

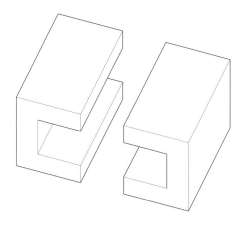

other than

To be outside a set or selection. This can be either positive or negative for the object or person outside. However, this state helps define the entity and the other group.

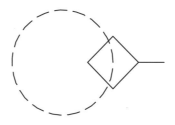

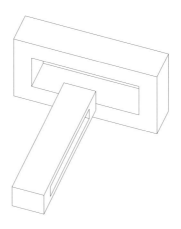

out of

To remove an element from a conglomeration or collection of others. This can help define the object or time leaving the realm or space of the other, but it does not define or describe the initial group.

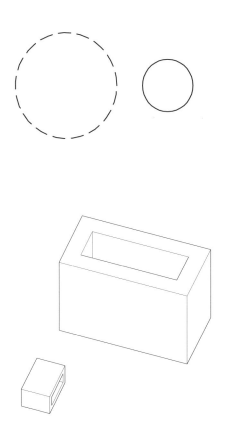

outside

To stand or move beyond the boundary of another. The center and its boundary are not defined in any way by the other. This other, however, is partially described by the boundary if in proximity or orbit.

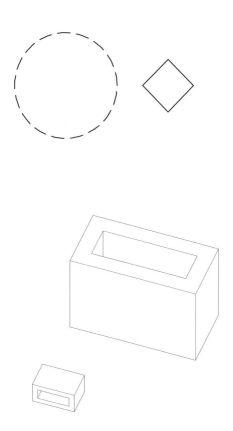

outside of

To exist beyond the boundary or limit of another. The definition of this element does not need to be similar or different to the bounded other, however an understanding can be drawn by the relation of the one to the other.

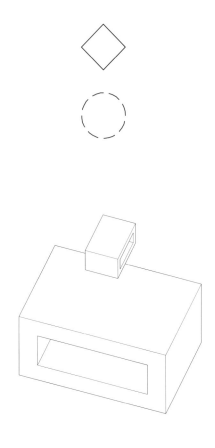

over

To exist or travel above another entity and define an advantage. The element above is likely to have some visual or spatial control of those below, however the lower entity or entities may not be aware of the condition.

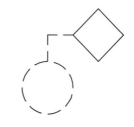

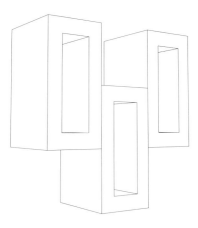

owing to

To produce a condition or entity through the operation on or by another. That produced cannot exist wholly separate to the other without defining it relative to that other.

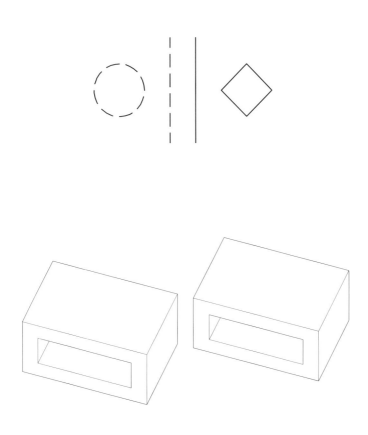

past

To move through and beyond a space or time, affecting the one progressing forward but the space or time behind remains effectively unaltered.

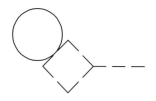

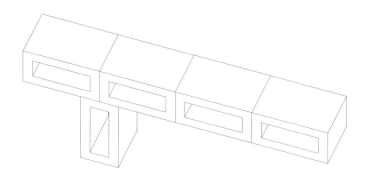

pending

To act or occur on the condition of some other action or state. The effect is defined by the incident, however the initial action or state does not necessarily have a relationship with the following conditions.

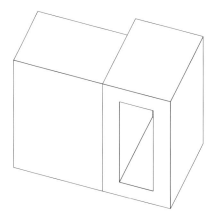

per

To define an entity through the specific relationship or actions of another. This other may not be described by the entity, however. This is a conditional relationship.

plus

To include another to create a greater sum or advantage.
The aggregation of the elements creates a whole that shares
characteristics with the parts but is something greater.

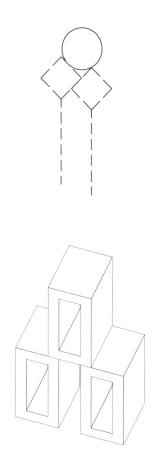

preparatory to

To define an order, to begin before others, and possibly to describe a causal relationship. The subject can control the meaning and nature of that which follows, and in this way, has a stronger position than to fall after.

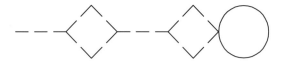

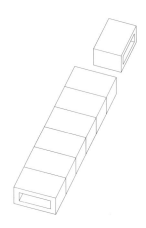

prior to

To exist or occur before something else. This can be a time or an experience in space. Both or all do not have to have a similarity other than the temporal or spatial relationship and grouping.

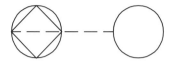

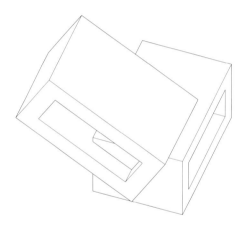

pro

To be partial to or in favor of another. The two do not have to share spatial or temporal similarities, but they must share a common objective.

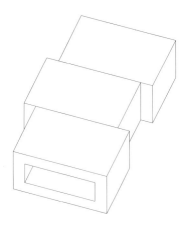

re

To describe or relate one thing or time to another, where the item compared may not have relation to the element described. However, the element regarding the other is described by the other.

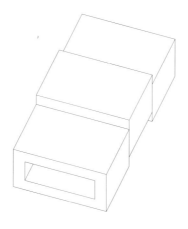

regarding

To describe through focus or study of or by another. A point of view is necessary for one to be defined in this way, and this entity is the object in view. A relationship exists between the two.

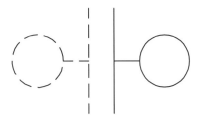

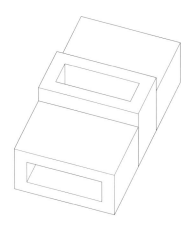

regardless of

To not count or acknowledge the interaction or change brought about by interface with another or others. This is a subtractive relationship where the subject is described and exists in spite of another.

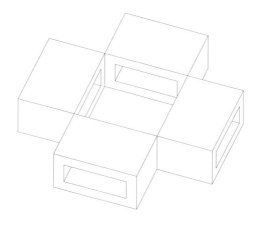

respecting

To describe an element through the perspective of another. The two objects or times can define each other, but one is minor to the other. The relationship is relative to the frame of reference.

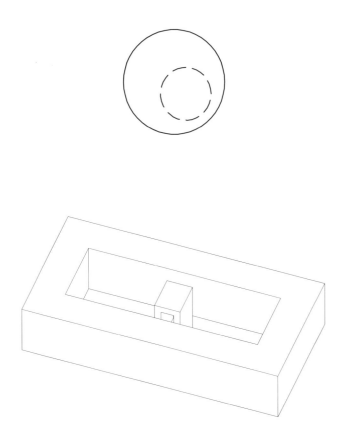

round

To be circling near or existing throughout an object, space, or time. The element near serves to describe the other, and the two carry major and minor roles in the system or relationship.

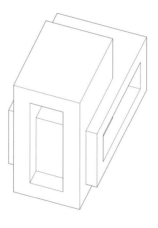

save

To remove one or more elements from an abstract grouping. The separation of this or these provides a new condition and definition of those removed, as well as those that remain in the initial group.

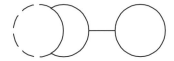

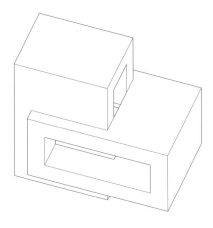

save for

To describe an element or group by the exclusion from another. The condition creates heterogeneity with differences peppering the whole or group, and the whole is redefined by this condition.

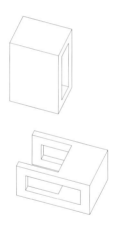

saving

To deny or take exception to another whether to hold or protect, or to remove or deny. Although the purpose of separating the subject from the other or others may vary, the description of the subject is through contrast.

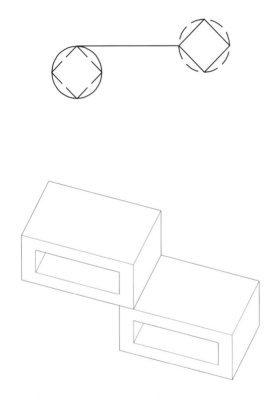

since

To define an entity from a specific action or point in time or space. The initial state allows the measure of the following condition.

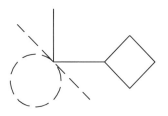

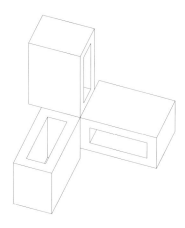

than

To relate two or more entities by comparing the similarities of these, but by doing this the differences are highlighted. The relationship of these does create an understanding of a group, but it is an aggregation of disparate parts, rather than homogenous.

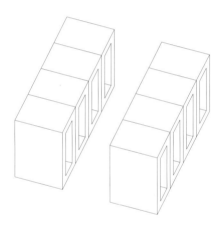

thanks to

To acknowledge the importance and effect of one in the transformation or growth of another. This relationship is constructive and points to the improvement or change brought by interaction and coordination.

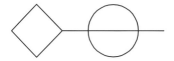

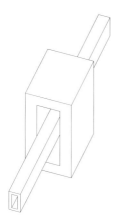

through

To pass from one side of a boundary to the other. Usually, this relationship partially defines the element passing, however the extent and form of the space being traversed may also be described with this.

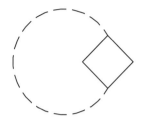

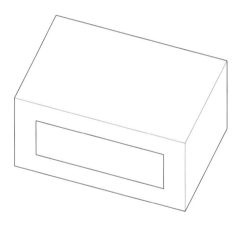

throughout

To exist consistently across time or space with a constant density or period of occurrence. The whole can be described by these elements, and the consistency creates an index or rhythm to play against.

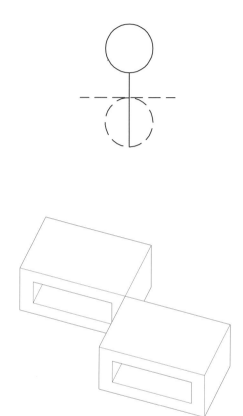

till

To exist in time or space to a specific moment or limit, filling and defining that length before the elements at the defined instance or boundary. The transition or absence is implied by the term.

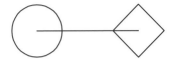

to

To head in the direction of another to highlight some similarity or condition. This is either a static center and a dynamic actor or two dynamic actors convening.

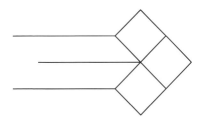

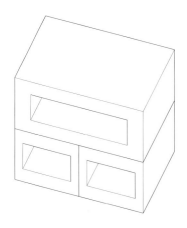

together with

To add an entity to another or others. By creating this grouping, the definition of the individual elements is given by the whole, where the description or nature of one can transfer to the others.

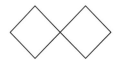

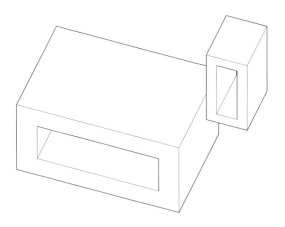

touching

To exist in a continuous space or time but defined as separate, discrete objects or moments. The separate entities may not have a relationship between or among one another, but they create a heterogenous aggregation.

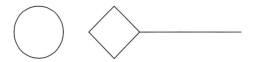

toward

To move or fill space in the direction of another. The element in motion or defining the volume is minor to the element that is the focus or in the direction of the other.

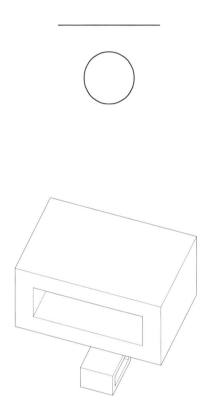

under

Move beneath or below an object or space to support, subvert, or subject. This relationship may suggest being controlled, but it may just be that it is in control.

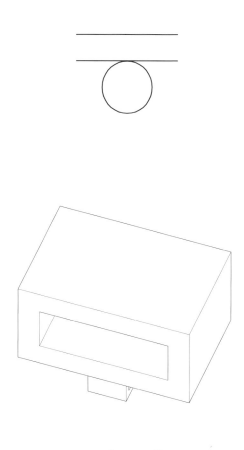

underneath

To stand or occur below something else. That above may not be aware of that below, however that above is apparent. The entity beneath, in this relationship, can act freely or affect the elements above.

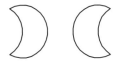

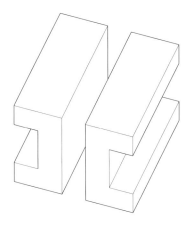

unlike

To describe one through the differences from another.
The relationship is not necessarily negative, but it is clearly
separating the two elements from one another.

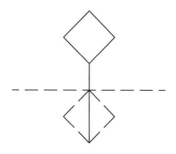

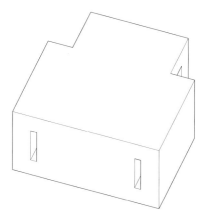

until

To define an element by the extent and limit of time or space up to a specific datum or boundary. A transformation occurs at this limit where the element's understanding or description changes.

up

To move or define space toward a point above. The change or direction can create an increased sense of importance or value, however an increase in effort or energy may also be implied.

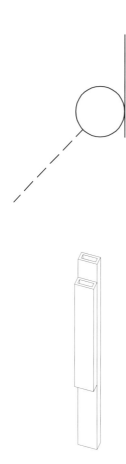

up against

To place an object, space, or time immediately adjacent to another where the understanding or definition of one may be transferred to the other. The relationship of these creates a whole that may be broken into disparate parts.

up to

To extend to the limit of an object, space, or time but not beyond, unless allowing a transformation. The condition defines both the entity and the specific limit.

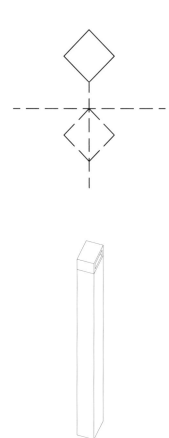

up until

To mark the limit or boundary of a time or space with the edge or envelope of another. The two adjoining entities remain separate, however both define the volume or length of time in focus.

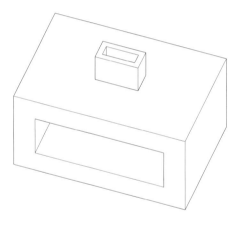

upon

To be on or move onto something or sometime where a difference in nature of time, material, or elevation between the base and the surrounds creates a separation. The condition implies some protection or change in meaning for the element on the other.

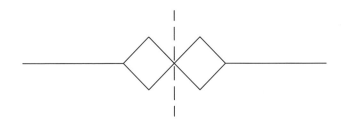

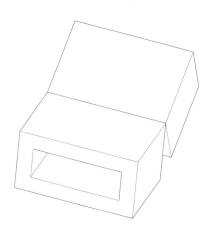

versus

To stand opposite another, creating a relationship that describes the dissimilarity of both but does not need to define the whole of either. The space between both is charged and important.

via

To express the method of use on or through some mode. The subject is a point or moment along some continuum defined by the mode.

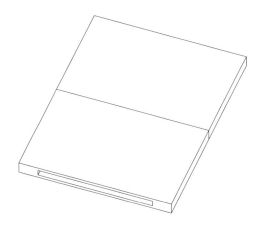

vis-à-vis

To relate one element to another to describe one or both. The conjunction of the two creates a relationship of both in opposition or combination. But both elements can be defined without the other.

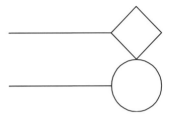

with

To be near and aligned to another. Both entities are described by this relationship, but there could be a major and minor position for the two of these.

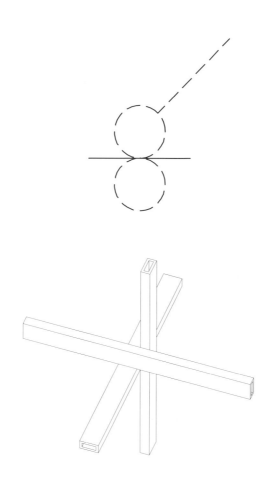

with reference to

To describe or allude to another where the subject is the major element and that describing is the dependent, minor element. One can exist without the other.

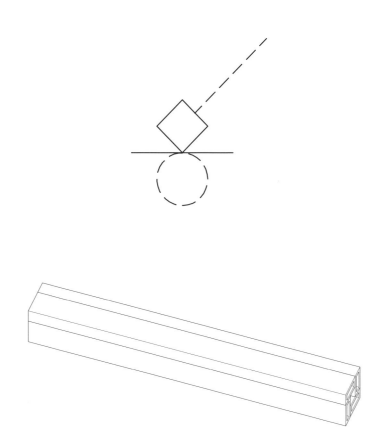

with regard to

To describe how one element concerns or is understood in respect to another. The perspective of one element defines the other, although this other may have a meaning outside of the relationship with the element.

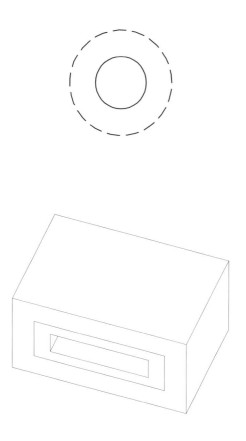

within

To exist inside an envelope or container which is evident and whole, creating a spatial or temporal condition completely separate and different the the exterior.

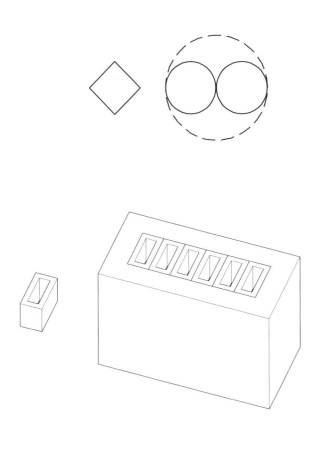

without

The knowledge that something or someone is unable to
be present with some other. This defines the state of being,
where the description is what is not, not what is.

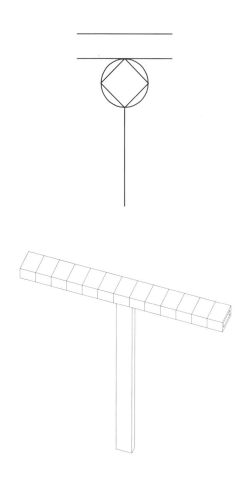

worth

To describe the value of something by another. This relationship allows the transformation of one to another by the description as a quantifiable amount.

A plane flew but for the cloud.
A plane flew by the cloud.
A plane flew by means of the cloud.
A plane flew circa the cloud.
A plane flew close to the cloud.
A plane flew concerning the cloud.
A plane flew considering the cloud.
A plane flew contrary to the cloud.
A plane flew cum the cloud.
A plane flew depending on the cloud.
A plane flew despite the cloud.
A plane flew down the cloud.
A plane flew due to the cloud.
A plane flew during the cloud.
A plane flew except the cloud.
A plane flew except for the cloud.
A plane flew excepting the cloud.
A plane flew excluding the cloud.
A plane flew following the cloud.
A plane flew for the cloud.
A plane flew forward of the cloud.
A plane flew from the cloud.
A plane flew further to the cloud.
A plane flew given the cloud.
A plane flew gone the cloud.
A plane flew in the cloud.
A plane flew in addition to the cloud.
A plane flew in between the cloud.
A plane flew in case of the cloud.
A plane flew in favor of the cloud.
A plane flew in front of the cloud.
A plane flew in lieu of the cloud.
A plane flew in spite of the cloud.
A plane flew in the face of the cloud.
A plane flew in view of the cloud.
A plane flew including the cloud.
A plane flew inside the cloud.
A plane flew instead of the cloud.
A plane flew into the cloud.

A plane flew irrespective of the cloud.
A plane flew less the cloud.
A plane flew like the cloud.
A plane flew minus the cloud.
A plane flew near the cloud.
A plane flew near to the cloud.
A plane flew next to the cloud.
A plane flew notwithstanding the cloud.
A plane flew of the cloud.
A plane flew off the cloud.
A plane flew on the cloud.
A plane flew on account of the cloud.
A plane flew on behalf of the cloud.
A plane flew on board the cloud.
A plane flew on top of the cloud.
A plane flew onto the cloud.
A plane flew opposite the cloud.
A plane flew opposite to the cloud.
A plane flew other than the cloud.
A plane flew out of the cloud.
A plane flew outside the cloud.
A plane flew outside of the cloud.
A plane flew over the cloud.
A plane flew owing to the cloud.
A plane flew past the cloud.
A plane flew pending the cloud.
A plane flew per the cloud.
A plane flew plus the cloud.
A plane flew preparatory to the cloud.
A plane flew prior to the cloud.
A plane flew pro the cloud.
A plane flew re the cloud.
A plane flew regarding the cloud.
A plane flew regardless of the cloud.
A plane flew respecting the cloud.
A plane flew round the cloud.
A plane flew save for the cloud.
A plane flew since the cloud.
A plane flew than the cloud.

Use of Prepositions in the Real World

In this work, we have discussed how to use prepositions and the possibilities of manipulating and changing meaning and construction.

In the first part of the book, we lay the groundwork, describing prepositions as a part of speech and how they function in language, reviewing the types of prepositions and examples of each. We understand that there are Prepositions of Time, Place, Movement, Manner, Agent, Measure, Source, and Position, and several prepositional words can fit comfortably in multiple types. Each of the types of prepositions can apply to architecture. It is clear that Prepositions of Time and Place are relevant, but the other six types fit well, too. The nature of these other preposition types allow the designer to be more creative, where a preposition type beyond Time and Place may need to be interpreted to allow a very creative solution. A new point of view or artistic license will allow new forms and relationships through the exploration and extrapolation of meaning of each of the prepositions.

In the next section, we explore possible relationships, defined by prepositions, from the small detail to the scale of the city. The preposition game provides a means to discover and reinterpret the design, structure, and form of an architectural intervention by superimposing our abstract and playful understanding through language on our concrete and practical development of a design. Here we have the chance to work with all eight types of preposition to allow a very broad array of possible relationships or operations. The use of each preposition will produce new and different results beyond the common or habitual means of design, and within this host of possible options, there are most likely several delightful or innovative solutions that appear simply through the introduction of a particular preposition or prepositional phrase.

After the preposition game examples, the next section gives an individual description for most of the prepositions in contemporary English. The description for each preposition is provided in diagrammatic, spatial, and verbal forms, and these varying forms provide meaning for the words while presenting an opportunity to vary or deepen meanings in the design to spur the designer to think creatively about the problem at hand and its solution. This section provides both a reference and perspective on the large number of possibilities in that there are over 140 prepositions described, and many of these prepositions have multiple meanings or understandings.

In the final section of the book, we have real world examples that highlight architectural innovations by looking at the problem slightly differently, and we use the preposition as the frame or filter to describe these. In truth, there are even more prepositions that can be used to characterize the form and architecture. We can say that the more viable prepositions that are possible, the more complex the design is, though a design does not have to be complex to be evocative and engaging. When reviewing the selection of prepositions in relation to the spaces and forms presented there are several levels of understanding you should work through. First, think about the viability of the applied word. Does the word choice align with your understanding of both the word and the space? Next, ask whether the preposition is the best choice or whether there might be a better option. The word provided may work sufficiently, but is there another preposition that can heighten the meaning or description of the space? Then, ask what is the best way to judge the possibilities. Are there metrics that you use to measure the quality of a design, and can those metrics be used to rank the preposition choice, especially if there are multiple acceptable word choices? Finally, think about what other design could use the applied preposition or those others offered as alternate solutions when analyzing the examples. How can you map the definition of the design and its associated prepositions onto your own designs? Can this be transported and translated to another project? The analysis of the preposition and the design evaluated can lead to the stronger synthesis of new architectural forms and details.

All of this is meant to inspire the reader to use this system and find new possibilities and relationships in design. The reader should question the aggregation and relationship of elements and explore through the substitution and elaboration of the preposition and its context in the sentence. Although we might believe that we have a firm grasp on possible design options, using this method presented provides many more possibilities and gives new ways at looking at the design problem.

Opposite:
Villa Savoye
1931
Le Corbusier
Poissy, France
Photograph by
Jean-Pierre Dalbera

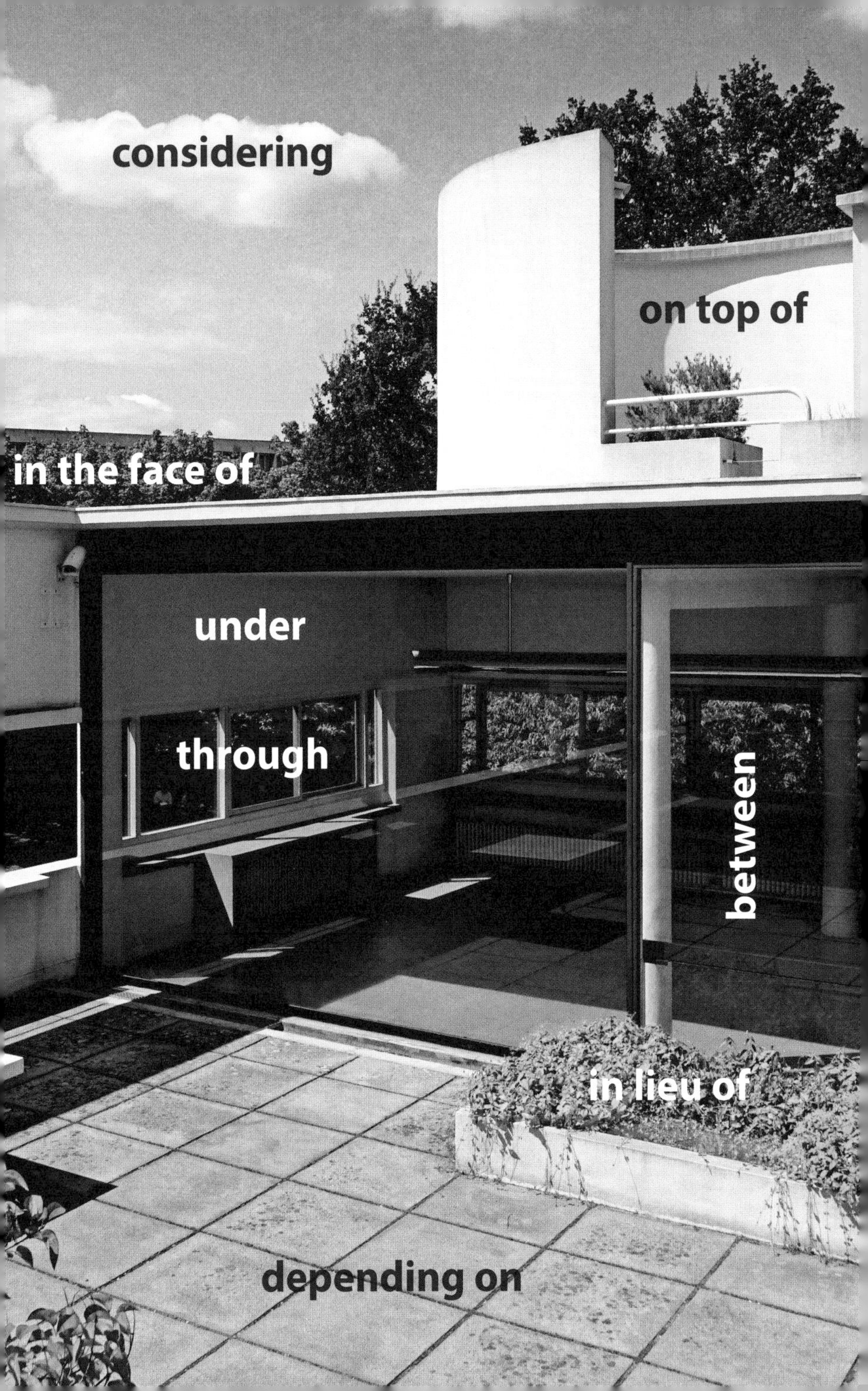
considering
on top of
in the face of
under
through
between
in lieu of
depending on

Opposite:
High Line
2009
James Corner,
Diller Scofido + Renfro,
& Piet Oudolf
New York, USA
Photograph by
Dansnguyen

in view of

among

in favor of

on board

along

above

Opposite:
Barcelona Pavilion
1929
Ludwig Mies van der Rohe
Barcelona, Spain
Photograph by
Rith

up to

notwithstanding

beyond

until

regarding

of

Opposite:
Wassily Chair
1926
Marcel Breuer
Dessau, Germany
Photograph by
Daderot

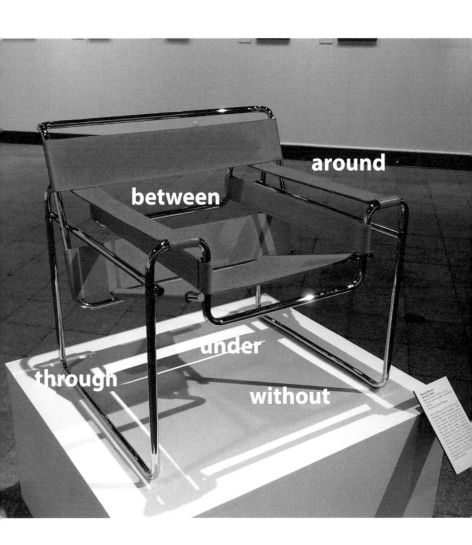

Opposite:
Central Park
1876
Frederick Law Olmsted
New York, USA
Photograph by
Carol M. Highsmith

other than

among

because of

inside

together with

Opposite:
Great (Bamboo) Wall
2002
Kengo Kuma
Beijing, China
Photograph by
Puku Puku

notwithstanding

with regard to

save

like

following

Opposite:
Fallingwater
1935
Frank Lloyd Wright
Pennsylvania, USA
Photograph by
Daderot

Opposite:
Map of Rome
1748
Rome, Italy
Map by
Giambattista Nolli

Opposite:
Das Haus Schminke
1933
Hans Scharoun
Saxony, Germany
Photograph by
Michael Sander

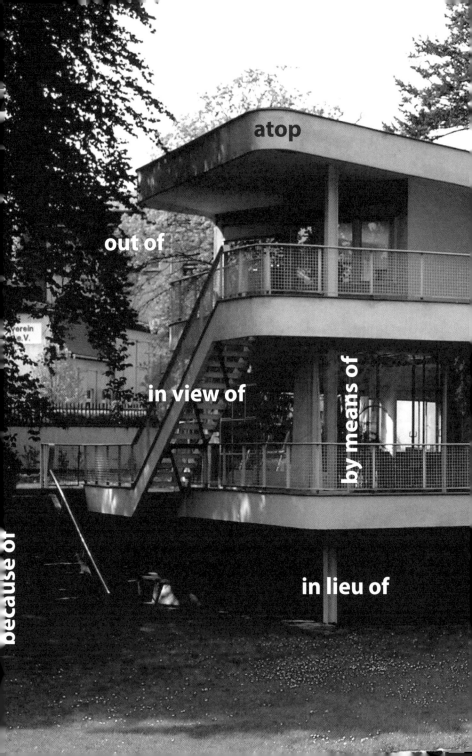

Opposite:
Guggenheim Museum Bilbao
1997
Frank Gehry
Bilbao, Spain
Photograph by
Xabier

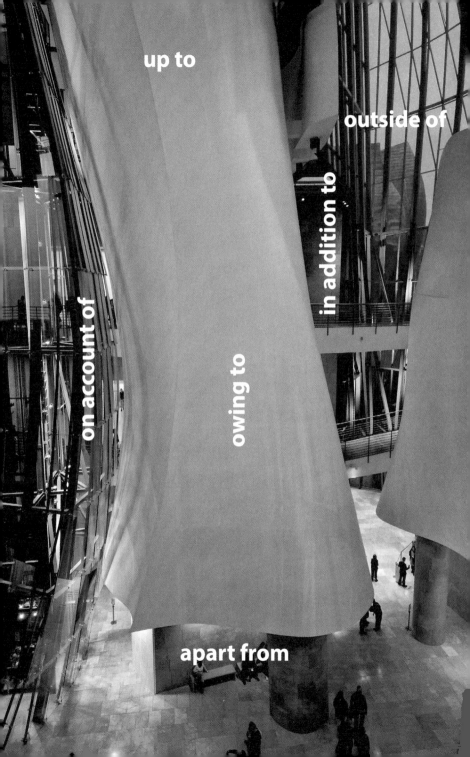

Opposite:
Heydar Aliyev Centre
2007
Zaha Hadid Architects
Baku, Azerbaijan
Photograph by
Sefer

Opposite:
Institute of Contemporary Art
2006
Diller Scofidio + Renfro Architects
Massachusetts, USA
Photograph by
Smart Destinations

in the face of

apart from

up until

regarding

in between

upon

before

Opposite:
Building
2006
Bjarke Ingels Group
Copenhagen, Denmark
Photograph by
Paul Wilkinson

Opposite:
Villa Tugendhat
1930
Ludwig Mies van der Rohe
Brno, Czech Republic
Photograph by
Timothy Brown

Opposite:
Art Institute of Chicago South Garden
1967
Dan Kiley
Illinois, USA
Photograph by
Ken Lund

within

among

on account of

in between

Opposite:
National Museum of Roman Art
1986
Rafael Moneo
Mérida, Spain
Photograph by
Anual

aboard

astride

vis-à-vis

toward

along

by means of

over

around

under

considering

through

Opposite:
Pompidou Centre
1977
Renzo Piano, Richard Rogers,
& Gianfranco Franchini
Paris, France
Photograph by
Gratuit

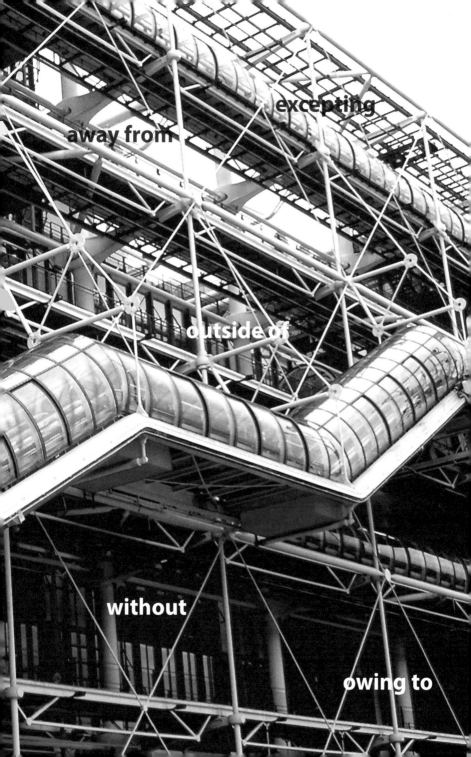

away from

excepting

outside of

without

owing to

Opposite:
Seattle Central Library
2004
OMA
Washington, USA
Photograph by
Jeff Wilcox

Opposite:
Noguchi Table
1947
Isamu Noguchi
Produced by
Herman Miller

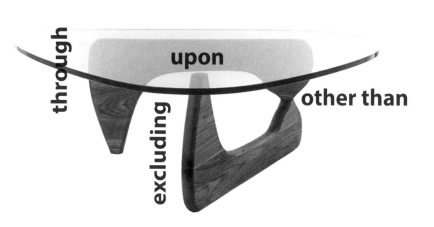

Opposite:
Therme Vals
1996
Peter Zumthor
Vals, Switzerland
Photograph by
Timothy Brown

Opposite:
Building
1661
André Le Nôtre
Versailles, France
Photograph by
Annette Beetge

other than

due to

versus

among

Opposite:
Vietnam Veterans Memorial
1982
Maya Lin
Washington, D.C., USA
Photograph by
Timothy Brown

Opposite:
Yokohama Port Terminal
2002
Foreign Office Architects
Yokohama, Japan
Photograph by
Forgemind Archimedia

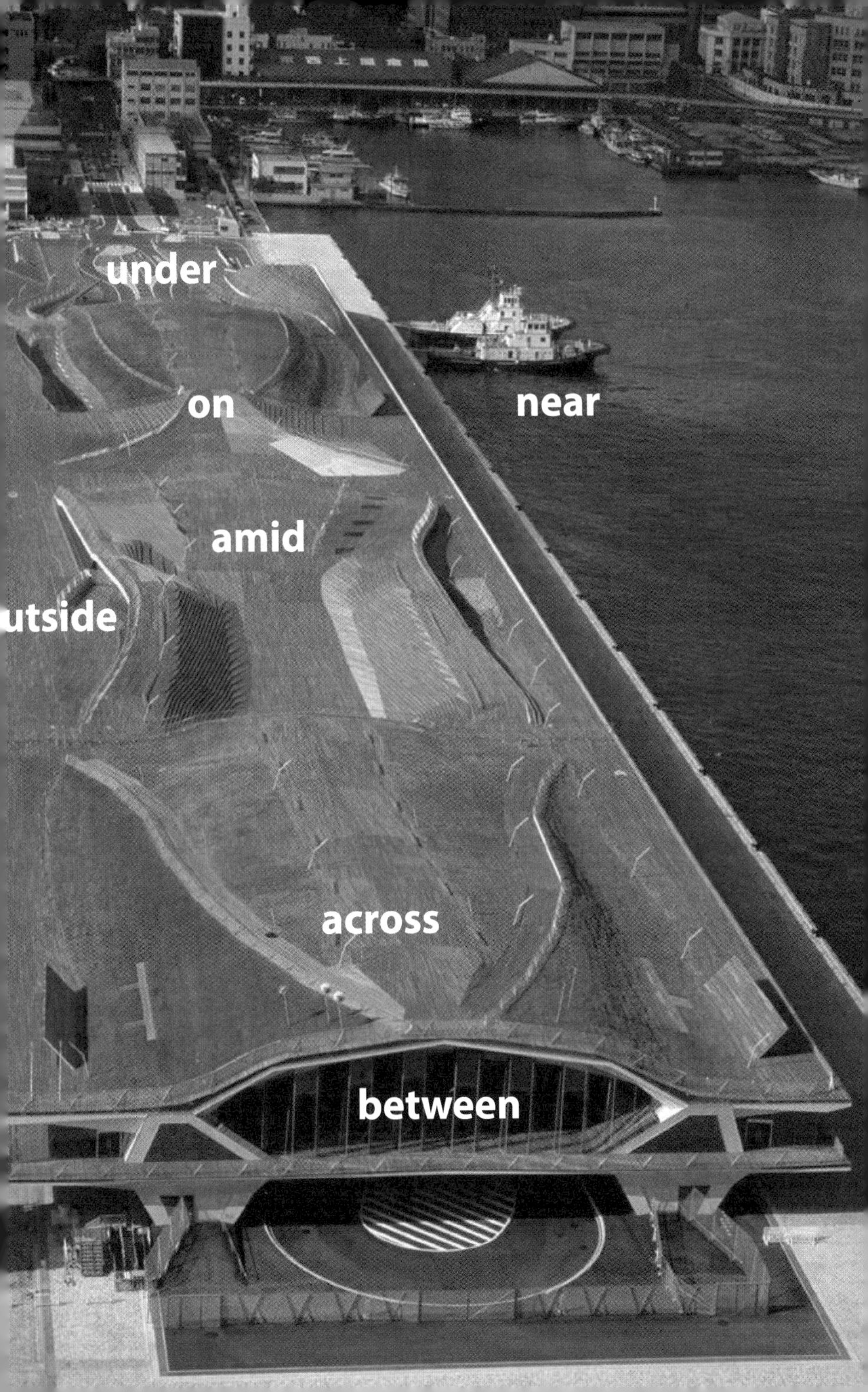
under
on
near
amid
utside
across
between

"Life goes on within you
and without you."

-The Beatles